Journal

Recommended Ages 8 through 13

ERIN C. MAHONEY

with RODNEY MILES, Illustrations by KEITH SEIDEL

Girl Power Go

"Somebody who has had Girl Power *is* strong."
~ Gaby, Original Girl Power Girl!

Copyright © 2017 by Erin C. Mahoney. All rights reserved.
Published by Girl Power Go, LLC
No part of this book may be reproduced in any manner without written permission except in the case of brief quotations embodied in critical articles and reviews. For information about special discounts for bulk purchases or author interviews, appearances, and speaking engagements please contact the author via: girlpowergo.com and info@girlpowergo.com
First Edition
Collaboration, consulting, editing, cover and book design by Rodney Miles:
www.RodneyMiles.com
Illustrations by Keith Seidel: www.KeithSeidel.com
Girl Power logo designed by Keith Weilding
All photo images by the author

Certificate border and ribbon © Can Stock Photo / kaarsten

WELCOME to Girl Power!

The workbook you now hold has all you need to complete the original Girl Power program designed by Mrs. Mahoney. And it doesn't matter if you are doing the program at home, in a group, or at school.

This workbook is yours! You can keep it and always look back on it and enjoy your time in Girl Power all over again!

Girl Power will always be inside of you!

For parents, instructors, and others who would like even more background and theory for an even richer Girl Power experience, Erin C. Mahoney has also published the *Girl Power Guidebook*.

Get ready! Get excited!
And let's get going!

For Danielle

This book is dedicated to my mother Danielle.
You were the strongest woman I ever knew.
Your strength, passion, and love live on inside of me.
They are in everything I do!

This book shares so many of the life lessons you taught me.
I miss you every day of my life but your spirit continues to inspire and bring love and care to others.

It's also dedicated to every girl and every woman who ever doubted themselves, ever felt afraid or alone; to every girl and woman that lacks self confidence, self-love, and the solid belief that they are powerful and strong even in their weakest moments.

I have been where you are and this book is for you!
You have everything you need within you already to be absolutely amazing!

Contents

Discovering **Girl Power**! 1

Step 1: Start! 9
Step 2: "Warrior Class" 17
Step 3: The Power of YOU 31
Step 4: Good Friends 45
Step 5: Love and Kindness 67
Step 6: Healthy Eating 79
Step 7: The Importance of Rest 95
Step 8: Review and Graduation 121

To My **Girl Power** Girls 128
"Somebody who has had **Girl Power** *is* strong." 134
About Mrs. Erin 140
Appendix: Affirmations for Cards 144
Appendix: Bracelets and Beads 162
Photo Album 165
Testimonials 182
Books by Erin C. Mahoney 193
Get More **Girl Power**! 195

DISCOVERING GIRL POWER!

Welcome and Introduction to Girl Power!

WHAT do you do when you see somebody being **teased** or picked on? What do you do if **you** are being teased or picked on? How **powerful** are we? How can we help other people be powerful, too?

If you really do **Girl Power,** and if you really help your new **friends** do Girl Power too, you will find out how to be **courageous** and brave, how to take care of yourself and still be kind and caring. And the **secret** is, all of that is already inside of you!

There are really **smart** ways to fix problems and smart ways to stop bullies, ways that don't hurt other people, too.

My name is Erin Mahoney, and I'd like to be your new friend. I started the **Girl Power** program in my home town in Massachusetts after I helped my niece Gaby, who you will meet soon (she, like me, is a character in this workbook).

Gaby was being teased on her school bus. And we had to think of something smart to do. A few kids on that bus were calling her a

DISCOVERING GIRL POWER!

"tomboy." Now, that's not too bad, but Gaby still didn't like it. So what do we do about something like this?

Tell the bus driver? Sure, but the other kids might not like you for getting them in trouble and they might just wait to pick on you until you're off the bus. Do we go and **punch** them in their noses? Maybe, but that could end up in a bigger fight, and either you or they could end up getting hurt, which is not necessary.

So how do we stop something like that and still feel really good about ourselves? And is there a way to stop other kids from teasing so they don't also have to get hurt or feel bad about themselves?

See, if that happens, they are pretty sure to just go pick on some other kid! Is there a way to make these other kids stop and really think about what they are doing? A way to make them stop without hurting them and still be **brave and courageous**, a way to have your own **Girl Power**?

We got a shirt for Gaby that said:

"I'm not a Tomboy, I'm an Athlete!"

Be Strong. Be Smart. Be Amazing!

and she wore it on the bus. The other girls felt silly and they stopped picking on her. They felt exposed! It made them think. *Gaby had been brave and strong, she had claimed her own power without hurting anyone*.

And believe it or not, later on, those same kids ended up being Gaby's **friends**, in a way. "Yeah, girls don't mess with me anymore," Gaby says.

Gaby has **Girl Power**, and **so do you!** You just might not know it yet. But even if you do know you have power already and you don't have these kinds of problems, wouldn't it be nice to be able to help other kids who don't seem to know it yet?

How good will that make you (and them) feel? Well, it will make you and them feel **great**!

And like I said, **Girl Power** is already inside you! This fun workbook and the **Girl Power** class you might be taking will prove it to you. And from now on, you can

DISCOVERING GIRL POWER!

be powerful and kind, just like Gaby.

You will know what to do in **strange situations** and how to **feel great** about what you did. Other kids will probably really like the things you learn how to do in this workbook, and don't be surprised if they start to follow you.

But no matter what you do with your own **Girl Power**, you can live your whole life **happy and strong**, knowing you have it and knowing you can help other people find their POWER, too.

So I am really, really, **excited** about this! I love seeing girls just like you discover and learn how to use your own Girl Power! **Are you ready?** Then let's get started!

I want you to really get into this and really have fun with **Girl Power**! You can always ask questions and share exciting things you learn with your parents, teachers or class instructor, and I love to get messages from my **Girl Power Girls**!

So let's start right now! Say these statements out loud:

Be Strong. Be Smart. Be Amazing!

GIRL POWER

"I AM STRONG!"

"I AM BEAUTIFUL!"

"I AM KIND!"

"I AM AMAZING!"

Great! Now say them again, even louder and stronger!

"I AM STRONG!"

"I AM BEAUTIFUL!"

"I AM KIND!"

"I AM AMAZING!"

You know what I say?

"Yes, you are! Don't let anyone tell you different!"

With love,

Mrs. Mahoney

DISCOVERING GIRL POWER!

Are you excited about Girl Power?

Great! Write down your thoughts or draw them here:

What will you do with more Girl Power?

Be Strong. Be Smart. Be Amazing!

Gaby has Girl Power!

Step 1: Start!

Getting Started with Girl Power

Part 1: Welcome and Warm Up!

Get Moving!

Girl Power was designed to get girls excited about being **strong, independent, self-confident and healthy**! Over the next several weeks, you will be given tools to make good friends, make healthy food choices, feel fabulous about yourself and your body, all while having **fun**.

You will learn life skills that will serve you well both in and outside the classroom, with friends, with family, in sports, and in every aspect of your life.

Let's start by getting **moving** and warmed up. Let's do some stretching, then some jumping jacks, and then we'll run in place or around the room. It's fun to burn off some of the **energy** we start with, and to feel our own **Girl Power**!

Meet New Friends!

If you are in a class with other girls, it's time to meet each other! Tell the class **your name** and about something you love to do, or maybe about your favorite thing, or just

STEP 1: START!

something interesting about you.

It's sometimes fun to share something about you that no one knows. For example, I love to collect glass eggs. I think they are beautiful and I try to see how many different ones I can collect.

The other girls will do this also, if you are using this workbook in a classroom, and if you're shy, the instructor can help so we all meet each other. If you are shy and using this workbook from home, try talking about interesting things the next time you meet **new kids**.

This may seem hard at first but be brave and it will get easier. It's actually a lot of fun, to challenge yourself by sharing things you like with new friends! **You can do it!**

For example, you just tell everyone what your favorite color is, or maybe the name of your favorite pet, or about sports you like. And if you're doing **Girl Power** on your own, think about your favorite things and things you like to do. It's good to get to know yourself, too!

Girl Power is filled with a lot of activities and a lot of fun. By the end we'll all be stronger and we will make

Be Strong. Be Smart. Be Amazing!

some *good friends* along the way.

"I Am" Statements

At different times while we are doing **Girl Power**, we will be saying (out loud) different "I Am" statements. These remind us all of how fabulous we really are!

Our instructor will let us know that it is time for "I Am" statements and we get to say them as loudly as we can in three seconds! We'll do a countdown, like when a *rocket* takes off, like "three, two, one," and then yell the statement. If you're doing Girl Power at home, shout out "I Am" statements whenever you feel like it! Here are a few more:

"I am smart!"

"I am strong!"

"I am amazing!"

"I am kind!"

"I am beautiful!"

"I am powerful!"

"I am brave!"

You can come up with your own "I Am" statements, too. And whenever we say "I Am" statements our instructor might say, "Yes, you are! Don't let anyone tell you different!" And you know what? **She's *right!***

STEP 1: START!

Create some of your own "I Am" statements and write them here:

_____

_____

_____

_____

Be Strong. Be Smart. Be Amazing!

14   GIRL POWER

Part 2: Activity

Self-Portrait

Name:_____ Date:_____

Draw a picture of yourself ☺

STEP 1: START! 15

Part 3: Fitness

Mini Boot Camp

A "boot camp" is what they do in the **Air Force** when they want to make soldiers healthy and strong. In this part of the class we'll divide up into different groups:

- One can **jump-rope**,
- one group can do a **zig-zag** course,
- and one group can do **hula hoops**.

Be Strong. Be Smart. Be Amazing!

We'll all do our own group for a little while and then we can all switch, so everyone gets to do each of the games and exercises, and we can keep switching that way!

"I Am" Statements

And you can't do too many "I Am" statements! We can shout out our favorite "I Am" statements as we have fun with the mini-boot camp, and we can try new ones, too. This time, try these:

"I am smart!"

"I am brave!"

"I am amazing!"

Clean Up

If we don't clean up, we make unnecessary problems and we don't feel as proud of ourselves. Cleaning up can be fun and it makes us **powerful**, too.

Part 4: Wrap Up

Now we'll **calm down** and get ready to finish our *first* step towards really getting our own **Girl Power**!

It's time to think about how great we did today, and what we can do better next time. This is how we grow and get more powerful. If we have any homework, it

STEP 1: START!

will be fun because we get to exercise and grow our *Girl Power*!

Greet Parents

And if we're in a class or a group, as our parents come to pick us up, we can tell them all about our **first day** at Girl Power, and we can show them the positive energy we have, and maybe even introduce our parents to some of our **new friends**.

First Assignment

Do one thing every day that makes you **happy**!

That's the homework for the first week and we carry that though the *whole* program!

Positive Thoughts

For the Week and Beyond! Read these positive thoughts every night before bed and every morning before your feet hit the floor!

"I can do **ANYTHING** I set my mind to!"

"I am **AMAZING** just the way I am!"

Be Strong. Be Smart. Be Amazing!

STEP 2: "WARRIOR CLASS"

Being Brave and Courageous

PART 1: WELCOME AND WARM UP!

LET'S GET ROCKIN'! Let's get our bodies strong, healthy, and *warmed up* by doing jumping jacks, by running in place or maybe running around the room, and then by stretching our bodies. It feels *great!*

Girl Power girls keep their bodies healthy and happy!

REVIEW HOMEWORK

Now we'll go over any homework we might have had from last time, and we can share any **happy experiences** we had this last week, too. And let's write down **FIVE** things that you did this past week that made you feel happy!

1. _____

2. _____

3. _____

4. _____

5. _____

STEP 2: "WARRIOR CLASS"

What it Means to be Brave and Courageous

Hey, yeah—what *does it mean* to be "brave and courageous?" We might have different ideas about that, so we'll discuss it now, but here are some things it can mean:

- Doing the **right thing** even when no one else does,
- Standing up for what I feel is **right**,
- Trying something **new and good** even if I don't feel comfortable with it at first.

We can all talk about times when we *were* brave and courageous, and this can be a lot of fun to talk about. Maybe for one of us this was a time we started at a **new school** and we didn't know anybody at first, or maybe we went into a dark room *even if we were scared.* Those are the kind of things "**warriors**" do—things they know are *right and valuable* even if they are a little scared about it.

But even if we are really brave and courageous, it's also important to not take dangerous risks! Standing up for a friend *is* brave and courageous but if we have to confront **a group or bigger kids** it might be **dangerous**, too. So in that

Be Strong. Be Smart. Be Amazing!

case, it might be brave and courageous to quickly go get an adult to help.

Safety is important, and staying safe is not bad, it's just smart!

INNER AND OUTER STRENGTH

In **Girl Power**, we'll learn how to be STRONG both "inside" and "outside," too.

Here are some examples of INNER STRENGTH:

- Being kind,
- Making good decisions,
- Getting enough rest and sleep each night,
- Being patient.

And here are some examples of having OUTER STRENGTH:

- Running and playing sports,
- Making good food choices so my body is strong and my mind is smart!
- Standing up not only for ourselves but for others.

EXAMPLES TO SHARE AND DISCUSS

Go over situations we all are likely to face, so we can think about or discuss how we can handle each of them. After you discuss or think about it, write down your answers to these situations:

STEP 2: "WARRIOR CLASS"

What do we do if there are three of us and one of us gets left out?

_____
_____
_____
_____
_____
_____

What if we see someone not being treated well?

_____
_____
_____
_____
_____

What if we see someone sitting all **alone** at lunch?

_____
_____
_____
_____
_____
_____
_____

We can all talk about times we have seen these things happen, and we can think about how we might handle situations in the future.

This *really* starts growing our **Girl Power**!

Be Strong. Be Smart. Be Amazing!

Part 2: Fitness

Are you ready? In this part, we practice some real **Girl Power** OUTER STRENGTH!

These moves are *powerful,* so *never ever* use them on other people unless we need to seriously defend ourselves or someone else. Got that?

Kickboxing

We'll learn what "on guard" means, and we'll practice our "warrior stance."

Feel Your Power!

WE have the **POWER** to protect ourselves, our friends, and our families, and even our house and pets and things. We should really *feel the power* as we practice and it's not only okay to *growl and let it out,* it's a good thing and super fun!

Remember!
(say this out loud!),

"I am strong, brave, and courageous!"

Basic Punches

We'll learn some basic punches:

STEP 2: "WARRIOR CLASS"

- **Jabs**
- Cross punches
- Upper cuts
- Hooks

KICKS

And now it's time to learn and practice *kicks:*

- Front kicks
- Back kicks
- **Roundhouse** kicks

KARATE PUNCH

We'll learn to do a good *karate punch* with confidence and **POWER**!

RECOVERY MOVES

Recovery moves are moves that allow you to catch your breath. They are a little slower and require less energy than speed moves. Recovery moves are also used to transition or change from one movement (like a punch or kick) to another:

- Shuffle in place,
- Speed bag,
- Jack it out (Jumping Jill's),
- Jack with a punch,
- Bob and weave,
- Jab towards the floor and over-head punch in place, left and right side.

SPEED MOVES

Speed moves increase your heart rate, burn more calories and energy and

Be Strong. Be Smart. Be Amazing!

make you fierce. It's important to sprinkle both recovery and speed moves into your kickboxing fun! Speed moves really increase our **Girl Power** because they are so intense!

- **Football** shuffle,
- Flurry with upper cuts as fast as you can while in a squatting position,
- High knees.

All of these exercises create a lot of **Girl Power**. We might mix them up or focus on certain ones. No matter how we do them, they add to our Girl Power and make us strong and powerful!

"I Am" Statements

And let's not forget our "I Am" statements!

"I am brave and courageous!"

"I am powerful and smart!"

"I am awesome!"

STEP 2: "WARRIOR CLASS"

Part 3: Activity

Face Paint – Warrior Paint

We'll use special **faint-paint crayons** for this cool exercise, *but be very sure to only paint your face—not your body or anything else!*

Otherwise, you can paint your face **whatever feel you want** your inner warrior to show or look like! If you don't want to paint your face or can't right now, **draw a picture** or help someone else!

Warriors are brave and courageous and stand up for what is right. They do the right thing when no one else does.

Wrap up with more "I Am" statements and cleaning up after all the painting!

"I am brave and courageous!"

"I do the right thing, even when no one else does!"

"I help my friends and others, too!"

Be Strong. Be Smart. Be Amazing!

Part 4: Fitness

Review and More Fitness

Now is a **great** time to review what we've done for fitness, and to do it *in face paint!* Include:

- Jumping Jills
- Kickboxing

"I Am" Statements

And now, while we do our fitness, shout out more "I Am" statements!

"I am fabulous!"

"I am awesome!"

"I stand up for myself and others!"

Part 5: Wrap Up

If you are doing **Girl Power** in a class or group, you might be able to go home in your warrior paint. If you're doing Girl Power on your own, ask your mom or dad about this.

Now think or discuss what the best parts of this step in **Girl Power** was today—what you (and maybe others) did really well and what might be done better in the next session.

STEP 2: "WARRIOR CLASS"

HOMEWORK

Each day through your coming week, do at least one thing that is happy, brave, and courageous. Make a note of some of them here:

- What I did that made me feel **HAPPY** this week:
  _____
  _____

- What I did that made me feel **BRAVE** this week:
  _____
  _____

- What I did that made me feel **COURAGEOUS** this week:
  _____
  _____

HOW ARE YOU BRAVE AND COURAGEOUS?

What makes YOU brave and courageous already? You might be surprised to find how brave and courageous you are. Write down **FIVE** (5) things that already make you *brave and courageous!*

1. _____
   _____

2. _____
   _____

3. _____
   _____

4. _____
   _____

Be Strong. Be Smart. Be Amazing!

GIRL POWER

5. _____
_____

GETTING MORE BRAVE AND COURAGEOUS!

Fill in these blanks:

"I feel brave and courageous when I am _____ _____."

"Doing _____ _____ makes me feel nervous and afraid, but I know that if I

_____
_____
I will feel brave and courageous!"

"When I _____
_____
I feel brave and courageous!"

"This week I will
_____
_____
to grow my Girl Power!"

STEP 2: "WARRIOR CLASS"

POSITIVE THOUGHTS ~ BRAVE AND COURAGEOUS

Read these every night before bed and every morning when you wake up!

"I do at least ONE thing every day that makes me **HAPPY**!"

"I Am **BRAVE** and **COURAGEOUS**!"

"I CHOOSE to be AWESOME"

Be Strong. Be Smart. Be Amazing!

"This is where I choose to be."

STEP 3: THE POWER OF YOU

Girl Power is Already in You!

Part 1: Welcome & Warm Up

Get Moving!

This time we're going to do something special to warm up, we're going to do **continuous motion**. This means we'll find a fun *pattern* to do with our bodies and keep repeating it. This is a special way of warming up that builds power, **Girl Power**!

FIRST: Start with your back to a wall, then walk forward and **touch your toes** as you go. Then turn around and **skip** back to the wall you started from.

SECOND: Now **bear-crawl** away from the wall, and **inchworm** back to it! Or, another way to do this is to bear crawl to the middle of the room, do ten (10) pushups there (using your knees is okay) and then inchworm to the far wall.

Have fun with it!

Review Homework

Let's go over our **homework** (if we had any) from last week. Remember what it means to be **brave and courageous**? Great! This week, we're really going to find out about the **POWER**

STEP 3: THE POWER OF YOU

of YOU! And now get ready for another rockin' week!

THE POWER OF YOU DISCUSSION

What does having your own **personal power** mean? Do you realize that even at a young age you have the **POWER** to influence others? **YOU** have the **power** to control parts of your day.

When you wake up in the morning you have a choice. Do you pull the blankets up over your head or do you toss them off and **tackle the day**?

It can go either way but **you** have the choice, the power! Think about it. If you pull the blankets up will your parents keep coming into your room and telling you to get up for school? Think about or discuss your thoughts for a few minutes.

If you stay in bed, what happens? Your parents get **angry**, you get cranky, and so on. Or do you get yourself out of bed, get ready, eat a **healthy breakfast** and head out with a great **attitude**?

If so, Mom and Dad are happy and you are happy, and you can now rock the day! This is the **POWER of**

Be Strong. Be Smart. Be Amazing!

GIRL POWER

YOU in action! Own it! Decide who and where you want to be and **GO THERE!**

Part 2:

Activity

Things I Love About Me Worksheet

I love that I am

_____

_____

_____

_____

I love my

_____

_____

_____

_____

_____

And I also love that I am

_____

_____

_____

_____

girl power

STEP 3: THE POWER OF YOU

And I love my

_____

_____

_____

_____

_____

I feel AMAZING when

_____

_____

_____

_____

You are AMAZING and SPECIAL because YOU ARE YOU!

"I Am" Statements

~

"I am Powerful!"

"I am Strong!"

"I am Smart!"

"I am Special!"

"I am Unique!"

Be Strong. Be Smart. Be Amazing!

36 | GIRL POWER

STEP 3: THE POWER OF YOU

Part 3: Activity

Power Bags

For this you will need

- 1 bag
- Sticker sheets for decorating your bag
- 5 or 6 sticky notes (more if you would like and have time)
- Markers and pencils.

Decorate your **Power Bag** however you want—you can use markers, pencils, stickers, even paint, whatever you like. Put your **name** on the bag.

On your sticky notes write down things you think are **amazing** about YOU and put the sticky notes in your bag.

Look at these sticky notes a lot! They will remind you that you have **POWER** to be amazing! And never let anyone tell you different! Be powerful!

Now tear out your **"Things I Love About Me"** worksheet and put that in your **Power Bag** as well.

"I Am" Statements

"I'm amazing because I share!"

Be Strong. Be Smart. Be Amazing!

"I'm amazing because I am kind!"

"I have POWER and no one can tell me different!"

Clean Up

Of course, we can be proud of how clean we keep our spaces clean, and we should make sure to have all of the markers and other things picked up and put away.

That's part of **Girl Power**, too!

Part 4: Fitness

While you do these next **Girl Power** exercises, remember:

The only thing that stands between the start and the finish of ANYTHING is YOU!

Decide to succeed and YOU will!

"Think it, Believe it, Achieve it!"

First, get an idea in your mind, then believe that you can do it, and then find a way to get it done!

STEP 3: THE POWER OF YOU

39

Be Strong. Be Smart. Be Amazing!

For example, if someone wants to run a long distance you must first decide to do it. Then you need to convince yourself you can. Put together a training plan to get to the finish line. Then, **RUN RIGHT TO IT**! Make it happen, achieve it!

Now line up against a wall and do the following things back and forth:

• **Skipping** down and back: Widen your stride here, really stretching the skip, and do this three times.

• **Long jumps** with arm swings down and back: Try to land lightly.

• **High knees** down and back.

• **Squat jumps**, 20 times: Remember, your legs will feel very heavy here, but try and push through, challenge yourself and know that YOU have the POWER to do it!

As you do this, feel your heart, notice your increased heart rate, and remember how strong your body is!

• **Single leg hops** in place 10 times on each leg: As you do these, think about how it feels. Is one leg stronger than the other? We are not *symmetrical* which means one side of your body is always stronger than the other.

Can you tell which side of you is the strongest? Your heart is in the middle of your body, which means it takes strength from your entire body! Use it wisely!

"I Am" Statements

"I am strong!"

"I have energy"

"I have a healthy body!"

Part 5: Wrap Up

Phew! That was a lot of exercise, and it feels *great*! You're awesome for doing all of that today! Can you feel the **Girl Power**? It's already in you—it's been there all along. Sometimes we need to bring it out and to learn to use it, that's all.

You should feel pretty good right now! You worked hard and did good things for your mind and your body. You are reaching your own **Girl Power**, the POWER OF YOU!

Be Strong. Be Smart. Be Amazing!

So if you're in a class, we'll talk about how the day went and if you're doing **Girl Power** on your own it's time to think about what went really well today! Maybe discuss it with your mom, dad, or instructor. But always remember:

- You have the POWER to make good decisions!
- You have the POWER to make it a *good day*!

And remember to read all of things you put in and on your **Power Bag**!

HOMEWORK

Your homework for this week is to practice the POWER OF YOU and look forward to sharing what you did to be fabulous next week!

POSITIVE THOUGHTS ~ THE POWER OF YOU

"I have the POWER to inspire others!"

"I think it, I believe it, I achieve it!"

"Nothing worth having is achieved without hard work and determination."

STEP 3: THE POWER OF YOU

Girl Power Bags ROCK!

Be Strong. Be Smart. Be Amazing!

POK

girl power

STEP 4: GOOD FRIENDS

And Navigating Relationships

Part 1: Welcome & Warm Up

Get Moving!

WARM UP with some stretching, **jumping jacks**, running in place (or you can do laps around the room), and then some more stretching. Feel your POWER!

Hula Hoop and Tennis Ball

If you're doing **Girl Power** in a class, we'll break into groups of two girls each. Both girls stand inside the hula hoop. One will bounce the ball and the other will try to catch it, *while both stay inside the hula hoop!* If the ball gets away, you both have to go get it, *while staying inside the hula hoop!*

If you're doing **Girl Power** at home or without a group, try this by yourself— it's a challenge and it's fun!

Homework

If you had homework, now is the time to go over it with your mom, dad, or your instructor.

STEP 4: GOOD FRIENDS

Overview

In this class, **"Good Friends and Navigating Relationships,"** you will be given tools to make good friends while being one yourself.

The things you learn here will be of good use to you for the rest of your life. You will learn to lead by example, and you will see that in a relationship with a **friend** you can be good to them while still being good to yourself (and others), too.

Part 2: Activity

Index Card Activity

On an index card, write down the **quality** you think is the most important to have in a good friend.

For example, maybe you feel being honest, trustworthy, funny, kind, or loyal is most important. Write down whatever you really feel.

Now discuss what you wrote down with whoever is helping you, and think of some **good examples**, too.

Be Strong. Be Smart. Be Amazing!

Your Top 3!

What are the top three (3) most important or valuable qualities YOU feel you have that makes you a good friend?

1. _____

2. _____

3. _____

Paper Crush Activity

- Tear out the **How to Be a Good Friend Sheet** on the page that follows.

- Now *crinkle it up!* Don't rip it, just **crush** it up in your hands.

- Now drop it on the floor and step on it! Really crush it down there with your foot!

- Now pick it up and look at it in your hand.

Let's pretend that this paper is your very best friend!

- Say "sorry" to it, even though I bet you would say you would *never* treat your best friend that way!

- So try to **carefully** open the paper up and flatten it out again. Try not to tear it and be very

STEP 4: GOOD FRIENDS

careful when you are unfolding it.

Did it go back to normal? Is it *exactly* the way it was before you crinkled it up? Is it clean and flat? No, it's not, right?

Even though you said sorry it's still somewhat wrinkled and perhaps dirty from the floor. Correct? The paper is changed just as our **friendships** are changed when we say or do something mean.

You see, once you do or say something that hurts someone else, no matter how hard you might try to fix it, sometimes you can't get it back to the way that it was, just like the paper.

Remember that our **actions** speak louder than our words, and Girl Power Girls should always think before we speak.

It is so important to be thoughtful and kind with both words and actions! That's what Girl Power Girls do!

Be Strong. Be Smart. Be Amazing!

50 | GIRL POWER

STEP 4: GOOD FRIENDS

HOW TO BE A GOOD FRIEND SHEET

Mrs. Mahoney made this herself, because these eleven things are things that she looks for in good friends. Read each one out loud and discuss them. Remember, to have good friends, you must <u>be</u> *a good friend! Here's how good friends treat each other:*

1. *Good friends **listen** to each other.*
2. *Good friends don't put each other down or hurt each other's **feelings**.*
3. *Good friends try to **understand** each other's feelings and moods.*
4. *Good friends help each other **solve** problems.*
5. *Good friends give each other **compliments**.*
6. *Good friends can disagree **without** hurting each other.*
7. *Good friends are **dependable**.*
8. *Good friends **respect** each other.*
9. *Good friends are **trustworthy**.*
10. *Good friends give each other room to **change**.*
11. *Good friends **care** about each other.*

Be Strong. Be Smart. Be Amazing!

GIRL POWER

This page left blank so you can cut out the cards on the next page! And so you can draw or write down your thoughts!

STEP 4: GOOD FRIENDS

Part 3: Activity

Good Friend Qualities Cards

Cut out and decorate each of your cards however you want! You can use markers, pencils, fun cut scissors, whatever you like!

1. A **BRAVE** Girl

   stands up for herself

   and her friends.

2. A **STRONG** Girl

   never quits

   or gives up!

Be Strong. Be Smart. Be Amazing!

GIRL POWER

This page left blank so you can cut out the cards on the previous page!

STEP 4: GOOD FRIENDS

3. A **LOYAL** girl

never leaves your side

and has your back!

4. A **FAIR** girl

listens to and sees both sides of a story

and treats everyone the same.

5. A **SMART** girl

knows that she's just right

just the way she is!

Be Strong. Be Smart. Be Amazing!

GIRL POWER

This page left blank so you can cut out the cards on the previous page!

STEP 4: GOOD FRIENDS

6. A **REAL** girl

believes in herself and speaks her mind

in a loving, kind way.

7. A **CONFIDENT** girl

stands strong and knows she is enough.

She also lets others stand strong too!

8. A **KIND** girl

cares about

people's feelings.

Be Strong. Be Smart. Be Amazing!

58   GIRL POWER

This page left blank so you can cut out the cards on the previous page!

STEP 4: GOOD FRIENDS

> 9. A **POWERFUL** girl
>
> lets her light shine
>
> on all of her friends.

> 10. A **HONEST** girl
>
> tells the truth
>
> and is sincere.

Be Strong. Be Smart. Be Amazing!

This page left blank so you can cut out the cards on the previous page!

STEP 4: GOOD FRIENDS

"I Am" Statements

"I am kind!"

"I am trustworthy!"

"I am loyal!"

"I am proud!"

"I am smart!"

"I am strong!"

Clean Up

Clean up all your supplies and throw away any trash so your supplies will be there next time when you want them and we make our parents, our instructor, and ourselves PROUD! Pride is a big part of your **Girl Power**!

Part 4: Team-Oriented Fitness Games

Tennis Ball Running Game

This is a very cool game where we place tennis balls on small cones on the ground (we start with just one at first) in the center of the room.

We'll break the group up into teams and one half of us will go to one side of the room while the other half goes to the other side of the room.

Be Strong. Be Smart. Be Amazing!

GIRL POWER

One girl runs to the cone and grabs the ball, then **runs** to the other side of the room where she gives the ball to another girl.

This girl then runs and puts the ball back, then runs to the other side of the room and high-fives a different girl, who then runs to the **cone** and picks up the ball. Get the idea?

Do this until everyone has handled the ball and then take a break.

Next we add **another** cone and ball in the middle of the room so there are now two cones and two balls, and we do this all over again, but this time each girl has to pick up *two* balls and hand them off, and so on.

When we've all done that, we add a *third* cone and ball and we do this all again with *three* balls. It gets to be amazing and **lots of fun**! The real object of the game is to cheer on your teammates as they go, and to see how fast and how well we can all work as a *team*.

Girl Power Girls often work together in teams!

If you are doing Girl Power on your own, **no problem**! You can do the same game, but instead of working with other girls just touch the

STEP 4: GOOD FRIENDS

walls at the opposite sides of the room instead. You'll build your **Girl Power** this way, and you'll be able to handle more and more stuff, too!

"I AM" STATEMENTS

"I am honest!"

"I am a good friend!"

"I am thoughtful!"

"I am beautiful!"

And don't forget to make up your own "I Am" statements, too!

_____

_____

PART 5: WRAP UP

Now is the time to relax a bit and think about all the good stuff we did today, and all you learned. What makes someone a **good friend** in your opinion? How can you be a good friend to others?

You have the power to be a good friend, you know! And you have the power to make good friends.

Part of that is doing the right thing, even when no one else does, part is making good decisions,

Be Strong. Be Smart. Be Amazing!

GIRL POWER

and always *thinking* before you speak!

HOMEWORK

Your homework this week is to **be good to yourself and others.** And try to do something this week that makes you a good—no, make that a *great*—friend!

To have good friends you must <u>be</u> a good friend.

POSITIVE THOUGHTS ~ NAVIGATING RELATIONSHIPS

"Food for thought: Once you say something and the words leave your lips, you can't take them back! Think before you speak."

"Be true to yourself and others."

"All things that bring us great joy require hard work."

"Good friends stand by you in all situations."

STEP 4: GOOD FRIENDS

On this page, write or draw your thoughts about how you can be a good friend!

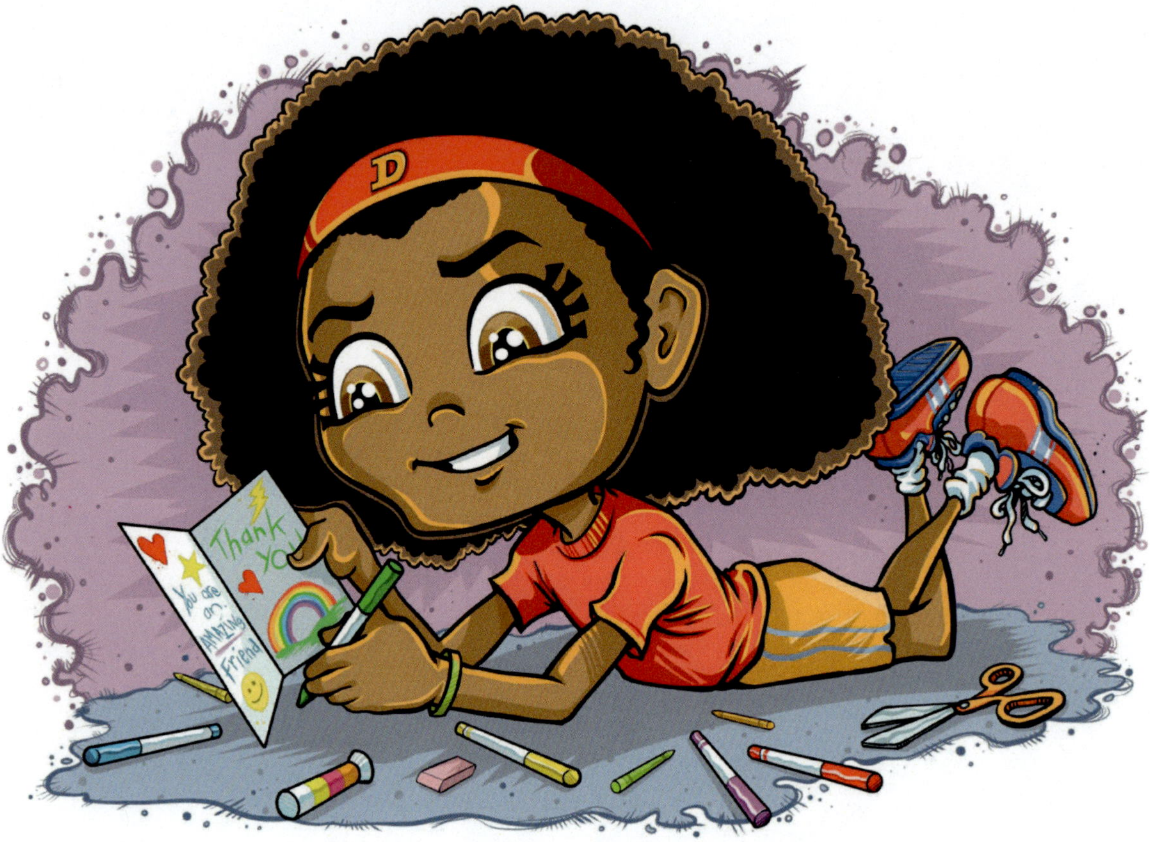
Thank You
You are an AMAZING Friend

Step 5: Love and Kindness

Including Random Acts of Kindness

Part 1: Welcome & Warm Up

Get Moving!

GET MOVING with **stretching**, jumping jacks, running in place or laps around the room, and then more stretching! Do this for three to five minutes.

Homework

If you had homework, share and discuss now! We can go over it together, and homework builds our **Girl Power**!

Part 2: Discussion

Love and Kindness

It's important here to be open and relaxed as we discuss what **love and kindness** means to us. We should be sure to talk about things we have done that really came from our hearts. Think about and share times you have given love and kindness recently.

Random Acts of Kindness Discussion

Do you know what "**pay it forward**" means? It means to do something for no other reason than because

STEP 5: LOVE AND KINDNESS

it feels **good** in your heart, or right in your mind.

For example, have you ever seen your mom or dad pay for a person's coffee in the drive-thru? Mrs. Erin, the creator of **Girl Power** does that sometimes. She surprises the person behind her by asking what they ordered and paying for it just because it's a nice thing to do. She only does it once in a while but it's fun and feels good.

Imagine how surprised and excited you might be if someone did that for you or your parents. Wouldn't that be nice? It's like spreading good **karma** to strangers. Maybe they will be inspired to do something nice for someone that day, too, and so on and so on! We have no idea how far our *random acts of kindness* might go.

Be nice to someone in your classroom that might be shy or quiet. See how it makes **someone else feel happy** and accepted, and then how that makes *you* feel. Invite someone new to sit with you at the lunch table or encourage your friends to be kind to kids outside of your current friend circle.

Be open to meeting others and accepting each other's differences. Be kind and

Be Strong. Be Smart. Be Amazing!

GIRL POWER

loving to your parents and siblings, too.

We are not alone, in fact others struggle with the **same things** at home and with friends that we do. It's all in how we look at things.

If you step back in a difficult situation and really try to view it in a loving and kind way, *it's never as bad or as big as you thought at first*.

It takes practice but it's worth the effort! And it also inspires others to be more loving and kind! Write down some of your own experiences to discuss:

I was kind and loving when I _____
_____
_____

And also when I
_____
_____
_____

I can be kind and loving next when I
_____
_____
_____

There is real **POWER** in **love and kindness!** It can help you to feel strong and confident inside. Splurge on it!

STEP 5: LOVE AND KINDNESS

PART 3: ACTIVITY

CARD ACTIVITY FOR "NO REASON"

Make a "love and kindness" card for someone you care about. This will be something we can do right now just to make somebody feel good, just to "pay it forward."

It feels good in your heart to do this, and you can do kind acts at anytime, for anyone, and feel good in your heart any time! How great is that?

Who are some people who support you every day but you might not always thank?

- Your mom?
- Your dad?
- Your brother or sister?
- A teacher?
- A friend?
- Maybe the bus driver or a coach?
- Grandpa or Grandma?

Wouldn't it be nice to say "thank you?" Wouldn't they be surprised? You bet they would! They'll feel **great** and so will you!

Make them an "I Love You" card, or maybe an "I Appreciate You!" card!

Be Strong. Be Smart. Be Amazing!

"I Am" Statements

"I am kind!"

"I am loving!"

"I am caring!"

Clean Up

It's kind and loving to clean up so the next people to use the space I'm in or use the stuff I use can also be happy using it!

Part 4: Fitness

Core Work

Your "**core**" is the middle of your body and includes your stomach and lower back. It's really important to make this area of our bodies strong, because then the whole body can be stronger!

Your core holds you up all day long, so it's important to exercise it in the correct way.

We'll **strengthen** our core by doing exercises both standing up and on the floor. It's a lot of fun!

STANDING OBLIQUE CRUNCHES

Stand up **tall** with your shoulders back and chest open, with your feet shoulder distance apart. Lift your left knee across your body and touch it with your right elbow. Do ten of these on one side then ten on the other side, too.

FORWARD BENDS WITH LOWER BACK LIFTS

Lift your hands over your head and reach for the sky. Begin to roll forward, keeping your back soft as you bend towards the floor. Hang like a **rag doll**. Feel the stretch. Straighten your back and point your tailbone towards the ceiling, with your belly button drawn in, and begin to lift. Be gentle and strong. Hold for a 10-count when parallel to the floor. **Relax** your back, round your shoulders and repeat three times.

STANDING TWISTS

Stand with your shoulders back and chest open, and feet slightly more than shoulder width apart. Your arms are tucked in along your side with elbows bent and knuckles facing the ceiling (**sky**). Hands are in a fist. Keeping your hips facing forward and abdominal muscles

Be Strong. Be Smart. Be Amazing!

engaged, twist from side to side. Be **strong** and resist in both directions. Feel the burn! Do for 30 seconds. Do two sets.

ACCORDION

Sit on the floor, on your buns! Lean slightly back and feel your **tummy muscles** engage. Now, with your knees bent, try to lift your legs. Your ankles and knees should stay together. Hands are on the ground on either side of your body to keep you balanced.

Then sit up and bring your knees in for a squeeze. Then release with your knees back to the starting position. Repeat this in and out motion for a 10-count. Then try to do a 20-count!

These exercises are a **challenge** but daily doses of exercise will make you strong and fabulous!

BOOT CAMP

Set up flat targets, low profile cones, hula hoops, and jump ropes. Put on music and go through an **obstacle course**! Be creative! While doing this, freeze at times and do 20 jumping jacks or 20 mountain climbers to keep it fun and interesting!

STEP 5: LOVE AND KINDNESS

Fun Running

Starting against a wall, we'll run when a **whistle** is blown:

- One whistle is run,
- Two is freeze!

Let's see who has on their listening ears! Then change it up or add a third whistle:
- 1 = run,
- 2 = freeze,
- 3 = walk,
- 4 = skip,
- 5 = hop on one foot.

"I Am" Statements

For this time, make up *all* your own "I Am" statements!

"I am _____!"

"I am _____!"

"I am _____!"

"I am _____!"

"I am _____!"

Part 5: Wrap Up

Ahh, what a session! That was a lot of **exercise** and a lot of good stuff we can do for other people, sometimes for no other reason than we like to make other people feel good! It makes us feel good, too.

Remember to "**pay it forward**" as you go through your days and nights, and

Be Strong. Be Smart. Be Amazing!

see how it makes people feel. What a great way to make the space happy around you. Do kind things when you see an opportunity or for no reason at all.

HOMEWORK

Let's discuss what you did last week that was loving and kind. I'm super excited to hear from you and how being love and kind or paying it forward made you feel.

This was your homework and as we know, homework and practice builds your **Girl Power**!

List **loving and kind** things you have done recently!

1. _____
   _____
   _____

2. _____
   _____
   _____

3. _____
   _____
   _____

4. _____
   _____
   _____

STEP 5: LOVE AND KINDNESS

Positive Thoughts ~ Love and Kindness

For the Week and Beyond!

"Strong body, strong mind, strong YOU!"

"Being kind to others shows how strong you are inside and out!"

"Do one kind thing every day for someone you care about. Being kind to others makes you feel great about yourself!"

"The greatest gift in life is love. Love yourself, love your family, and love your friends!"

Be Strong. Be Smart. Be Amazing!

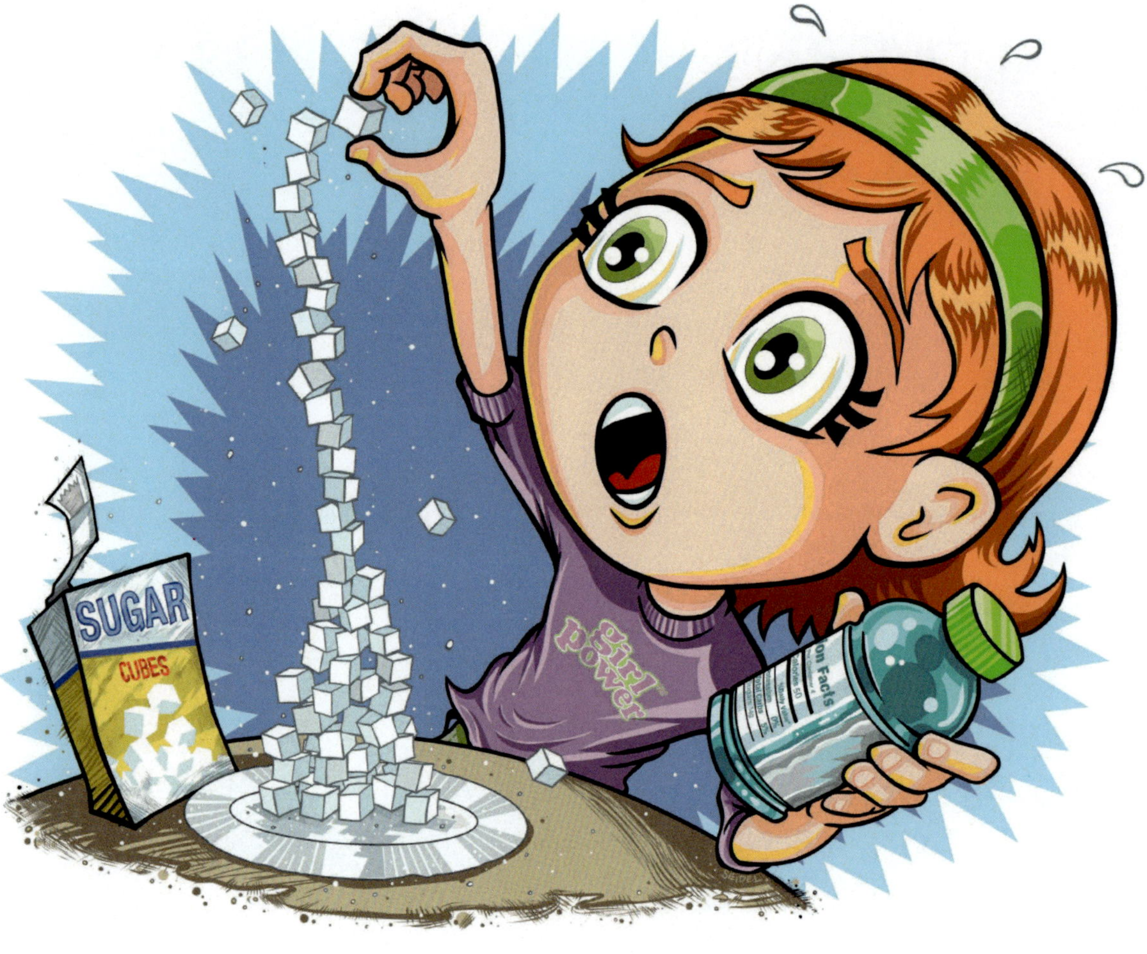
SUGAR
CUBES
girl power

Step 6: Healthy Eating

Habits that Last a Lifetime

Part 1: Welcome & Warm Up

GET MOVING with stretching, *jumping jacks*, running in place or laps around the room, and then more stretching! Do this for three to five minutes.

Homework

If you had homework, share and discuss now! We can go over it together.

Homework builds our **Girl Power**!

Part 2: Discussion

Food as Fuel

Food *is* what our bodies and minds use as fuel, and if we make good, healthy (and tasty) food choices throughout the day, we have FUEL for our **Girl Power**!

But how do you think about food right now? Do you like it? Do you not like the things you are given to eat?

And *why* do we eat, do you know? What does food do for our **bodies**? How do you feel after you eat?

STEP 6: HEALTHY EATING

What kinds of things are you eating lately? Share what your **favorite foods** are with the class or whoever is helping you with **Girl Power**, and share what your *least* favorite foods are, too.

Foods I Like!

1. _____
2. _____
3. _____

Foods I Don't Like!

4. _____
5. _____
6. _____

Fruits, vegetables, nuts, grains, dairy and water all have important roles in a balanced diet and healthy lifestyle.

If you put **good** things in, you get good things out! Strong bodies are the result of healthy eating.

Healthy snacking helps girls run faster and play harder for longer periods of time.

Your brain works better when it has healthy levels of nutrients. You can solve problems more efficiently and do better in school with a balanced diet, too.

Be Strong. Be Smart. Be Amazing!

Breakfast really is the most important meal of the day. It gets your **metabolism** going. "Metabolism" is when your body takes the food you give it and makes ENERGY. It fires your body up for the day and helps you to feel strong and fabulous!

What do you eat for **breakfast**?

_____
_____

How do you feel about food?

_____
_____

Food is **fuel** to our bodies like gas is fuel to our cars. It will take you places but only so far if you don't fill your tank with good nutritious foods throughout the day!

When it comes to snacking, have something healthy **first**. If you are still hungry then have a salty, crunchy, or sweet treat **second**.

Planning ahead is key when you are playing **sports** or rushing to music lessons, dance lessons or hanging out with friends.

"I usually snack on:

_____
_____"

STEP 6: HEALTHY EATING

FUELING FOR SPORTS

There is a way to get the most out of your body when playing sports, and that is "hydrate, hydrate, hydrate!"

That means to drink a lot of water—not all at once, but throughout your day or game or practice.

If you prefer sports drinks water them down. Most sports drinks contain way too much sugar—much more sugar than you might realize. But you can cut the sugar content by adding water to your sports drinks.

HEALTHY SNACKING OPTIONS

Plain water with a banana is great fuel!

Greek or regular yogurt and a handful of almonds or walnuts after a workout or training is a great combination.

An apple with peanut or sun butter is great!

Carrots, cucumbers, grapes and pretzels are all easy to pack and take with you.

Good "starters" would be apples; oranges; a banana; celery with peanut, Sun, or almond butter; carrots; raw

Be Strong. Be Smart. Be Amazing!

green beans or snap peas; grapes; berries; and yogurt.

All of these **healthy** snacks are easy to pack and travel with. They are great for energy before sports and will nourish your body while you exercise and play!

Still hungry? Enjoy any of the following crunchy, slightly salty, or sweet snacks that are still low in sugar but satisfy:

- Homemade **brown** rice tortilla chips or air-popped popcorn
- Pretzels
- **Fruit** kabobs with mini marshmallow's and your favorite fruits

PART 3: ACTIVITIES

FAVORITE FRUITS & VEGGIES WORKSHEET

List your top 3 favorite veggies:

1. _____

2. _____

3. _____

Now list your top 3 favorite fruits:

1. _____

2. _____

3. _____

STEP 6: HEALTHY EATING

DRAW SOME OF YOUR FAVORITE FRUITS AND VEGGIES!

Now, share what your **favorites** are and why. Listen as other girls and the person helping you with **Girl Power** tell you about some of theirs too.

Many girls like and dislike the same things—it's amazing! But what seemed to be your favorite? **Green** fruits and veggies? **Red**? **Yellows**?

This coming week, mix it up and try some NEW fruits and veggies. Some you might not like, but you might even find new favorites! Eating different color **fruits and veggies** is not only fun, it's healthy, too!

Be Strong. Be Smart. Be Amazing!

"Healthy Competition" Family Food Challenge

Let's make a food chart that you can use this week to do a healthy food challenge with **your family**!

You can do this on a large poster board or you can use the chart on the pages that follow.

If you're making your own poster board chart:

1. FIRST, draw a horizontal line for each family member in your household that will play (and don't forget **yourself**!).

2. NEXT draw a column from top to bottom for every day of the week starting tomorrow. For example, if your class meets on Thursday afternoons you should start the week on your chart with Friday.

Now that the chart is made, **decorate** it! You should now track the weekly total for each person.

Every time someone in the house has a fruit or veggie they earn a tally mark on the chart.

At the end of the week add up the tally marks. The person with the most tally

STEP 6: HEALTHY EATING

marks for healthy foods on the chart might win a prize or get to pick a family activity. Make it fun!

And you should know something about serving sizes. Here are some examples:

- A cup of **grapes** versus a single grape is what earns a tally mark!

- Although juices like **orange** and **apple** have *natural* sugar they are still *high* in sugar. It's important not to have too much sugar each day. so I suggest only 1 to 2 servings of juice per day.

How do we know if a serving is a cup without measuring anything? We can say that a "cup" is roughly the size of a tennis ball. That is a good guide.

- Servings of **salad** are tallied by the cup. You may **not** count each fruit or veggie in the salad as a tally mark!

Be Strong. Be Smart. Be Amazing!

"Healthy Competition"

Family Member	Day: _____	Day: _____	Day: _____
Name: _____			
Name: _____			
Name: _____			
Name: _____			
Name: _____			
Name: _____			
Name: _____			

STEP 6: HEALTHY EATING

Food Challenge Chart

Day: _____	Day: _____	Day: _____	Day: _____	Totals

Be Strong. Be Smart. Be Amazing!

Clean Up

Always important to clean up after making your chart, and especially when we work with **food**! Keeping your kitchen at home clean will make everyone happy, be healthier, and makes it easy to go in there and make up some tasty snacks!

What NEW, tasty, healthy snacks might you try?

_____
_____
_____
_____
_____

Part 4: Fitness

Circle to Circle

With your group or your instructor, form a **circle** by holding hands. You are like a chain conducting an electrical current. Start by lifting your hand which brings up the hand of the next girl in the circle. Continue all the way around the circle. Do you feel connected to each other?

Once you get the "current" to travel around the circle a few times, disconnect one set of hands. Add a **hula hoop** and reconnect them. The game just got more

STEP 6: HEALTHY EATING

fun and slightly complicated!

The purpose is to work together and get the hula hoop all the way around the circle without breaking the chain. You will have to work **together** to maneuver the hula hoop over and around each girl in the chain!

If there is time, **blindfold** one of the girls and do it again with the hula hoop, working as a team to guide the girl that has lost her vision with the blindfold.

"I Am" Statements

"I am a team player!"

"I am connected!"

"I am a problem solver!"

"I am smart!"

Part 5: Wrap Up

Time for some **positive feedback** about the class! Remember to make healthy food choices to keep yourself feeling **fabulous** and **energized**.

Homework

Use the **food chart** you created to mark down how many fruits and how many vegetables you eat each day for the coming week. You should challenge your

Be Strong. Be Smart. Be Amazing!

family to eat healthy this week as well, after all it is a "Family Healthy Eating Challenge!"

If you are doing **Girl Power** at home don't forget to talk about the Healthy Eating Food Chart and celebrate a healthy week!

Positive Thoughts ~ Healthy Eating

Healthy Eating that will last a lifetime

"You have ONE body, take care of it!"

"Exercise and healthy eating give you the power and focus to do AMAZING things!"

"What you put in is what you get out, so put healthy foods in and get amazing results out!"

"Know that your body is changing but it is just as it should be right now! Love every stage!"

STEP 6: HEALTHY EATING

MAKE NOTES OR DRAWINGS HERE!

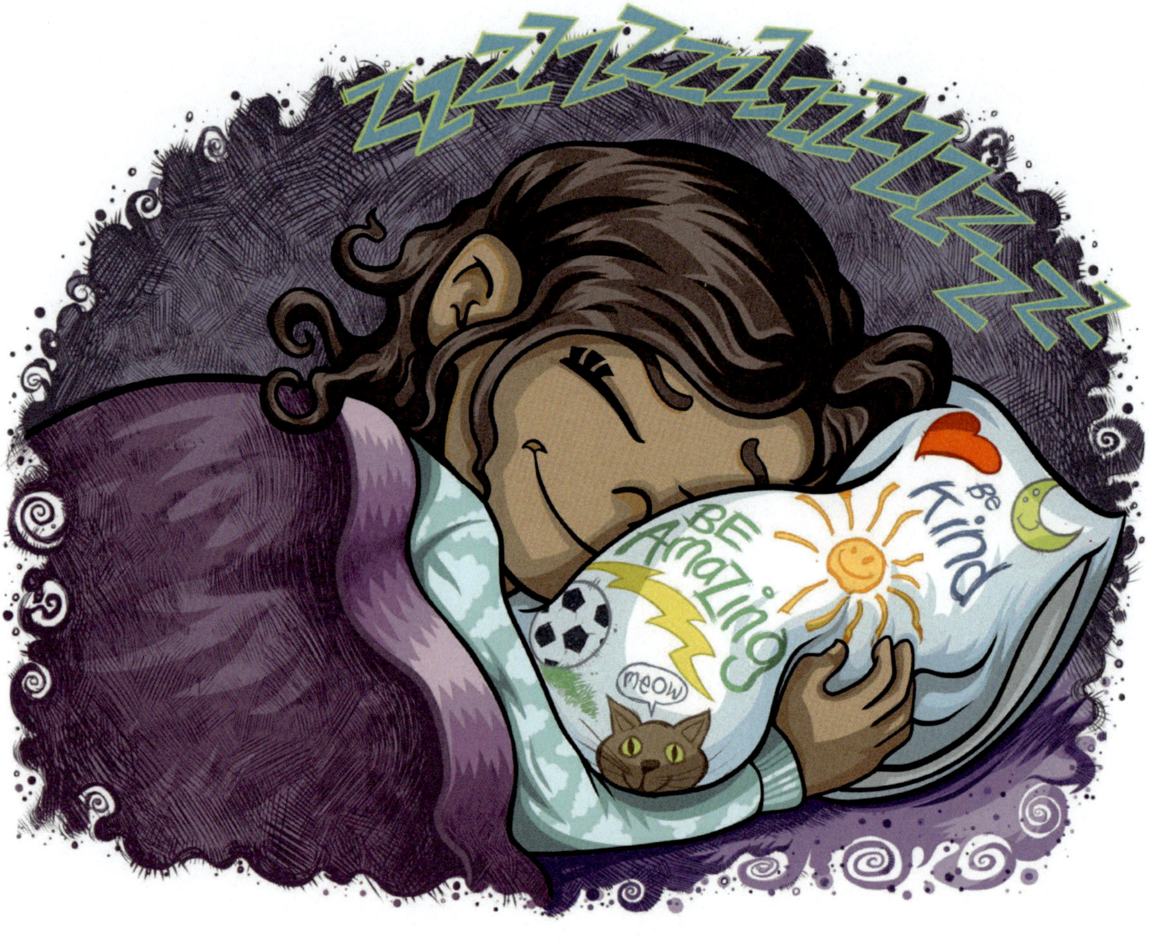
Be Kind
BE Amazing
meow

Step 7: The Importance of Rest

And an Introduction to Yoga!

Part 1: Welcome & Warm Up

Get Moving!

Let's start with more stretching than before because we are going to be doing **YOGA**!

Yoga is a way of moving your body into different positions while you control your breathing. It relaxes, strengthens, and develops your **strength**, **flexibility**, and even your **mind**.

You get stronger, healthier, burn off stress and become more relaxed. You get mega-**Girl Power**! But first, let's do five to ten minutes of **stretching** to warm up!

Homework

Did anyone bring back their food charts? How did the challenge go at home? How did you do? Did you have a super **Girl Power** healthy eating week?

STEP 7: THE IMPORTANCE OF REST

PART 2: DISCUSSION

SLEEP PATTERN

Let's talk about your **bedtime** routine:

What time do you go to sleep at night? _____

Is it different on school nights and weekends? _____

Do you go to be at 7:30, 8, 8:30, 9, 9:30 or later on school nights? _____

Do you go to bed later on weekends? _____

Do you do anything to "settle down" on a regular basis before going to bed? Examples might be that you read before bed either alone or with a parent, or maybe you take a relaxing bath, or play a quiet game.

Write down some things about your "bedtime routine" and how you like it here:

_____
_____
_____
_____
_____
_____

What about your morning or wake-up routine? Do

Be Strong. Be Smart. Be Amazing!

you wake up at 6, 6:30, 7, 7:30 or another time? _____
_____

Do you have a way you like to wake up each morning, maybe with your dog or maybe there's a way your mom or dad gets you up that you like or don't like?

Write about it here:
_____
_____
_____
_____
_____
_____
_____
_____

It's important to slow down at night to transition to sleep. This week you should try to establish a **relaxing bedtime routine**. This is part of your homework for the week.

People have figured out how much sleep we need to be full of **energy** and **powerful** all day long.

The following are standards for sleep in children according to people who have studied sleep:

- Ages 3-6: 10-12 hours per day
- Ages 7-12: 10-11 hours per day

STEP 7: THE IMPORTANCE OF REST

- Ages 12-18: 8-9 hours per day

What is your age, and which amount of sleep does the chart suggest you should have?

My Age:

_____

Hours of Sleep I Need:

_____

The proper amount of rest is critical for girls because we develop and grow while we sleep.

Brain function and the growth of our muscles and bones takes place when the body is at rest, therefore:

Proper rest is an absolute must to be really healthy and active.

Keep track of your sleep patterns this week and use the **Feeling Faces Worksheet** on the next page so you can track how you feel with and without proper sleep!

Another great way to boost our **Girl Power!**

Be Strong. Be Smart. Be Amazing!

Sleep Pattern Worksheet

Also known as the "**Feeling Faces Worksheet**," highlight the face (happy/sad/other) that shows how you feel.

Night (Monday, Tuesday, etc.)	Lights Out	Wake Up	Feeling (Happy/Sad/Other)
_____	__:__ p.m.	__:__ a.m.	😊 ☹ ○
_____	__:__ p.m.	__:__ a.m.	😊 ☹ ○
_____	__:__ p.m.	__:__ a.m.	😊 ☹ ○
_____	__:__ p.m.	__:__ a.m.	😊 ☹ ○
_____	__:__ p.m.	__:__ a.m.	😊 ☹ ○
_____	__:__ p.m.	__:__ a.m.	😊 ☹ ○
_____	__:__ p.m.	__:__ a.m.	😊 ☹ ○

STEP 7: THE IMPORTANCE OF REST

PART 3: ACTIVITIES

PILLOW CASES

For this exercise, you'll need:

- One pillowcase,
- Fabric markers, and
- One sheet of poster board to slip inside the pillowcase while you are working. This will prevent markers from bleeding through and allow you to decorate both sides.

Decorate your **pillowcase** however you would like. Once you have completed your projects, share what you have created!

CLEAN UP

Make sure all your markers are put away and that you've thrown away or put away your poster board, and that your newly **decorated** pillowcase is somewhere safe!

Be Strong. Be Smart. Be Amazing!

Part 4: Fitness/Yoga

Let's do some yoga!

First, remove your shoes. We'll begin with standing postures, which are called "**asanas**" or "poses."

As we do yoga, always be sure you are being safe and always protecting your body's joints and your back.

Today's routine will begin with **standing** postures, moving into **balance** postures. **Bending** poses are very nourishing and should be done at the end, followed by rest.

We'll start with a basic sequence of postures and we'll finish with **relaxation** and **meditative** or **rest** postures.

There are many benefits to **YOGA** for kids. It can help develop your body, your brain, your self-esteem and your emotional health.

Yoga can also help kids cope with stress and sharpen your awareness. It can help you become more creative and calm. But it's just as important to be sure to keep yoga safe, fun, and simple.

Let's do some **yoga**!

STEP 7: THE IMPORTANCE OF REST

Standing and Strength Poses

Mountain

Also called "Tadasana," this pose has you mimic a mountain by standing tall and steady. This is a basic starting pose for many standing poses in yoga.

1. Focus on grounding your feet into the floor and having the top of your head reach through the ceiling!
2. Your shoulders are back, and your chest open with good posture and breathing.

Be Strong. Be Smart. Be Amazing!

Warrior I

Also called "Virabhadrasana I," this is a focusing and strengthening pose, meant to build a connection, grounding you with the Earth's energy:

1. Start standing in Mountain Pose, then jump your feet out or step them out.
2. Place your hands on your hips and turn your right leg and foot out by 90 degrees. Your right heel should be directly opposite the inner arch of your left foot.
3. Turn your left leg and foot in by about 45 degrees.
4. Take a moment to make sure you are balanced, focusing your attention on the floor beneath you.
5. Turn your chest to the right.
6. Press your left hip forward in order to square your hips.
7. On your next inhale, raise your arms above

STEP 7: THE IMPORTANCE OF REST

your head and bring your palms together.

8. Gaze straight ahead and focus on the power of the pose.
9. Exhale and bend your right knee to a 90-degree angle. Your knee should be right over your ankle.
10. Take a moment to balance your body, pressing your weight into your right thigh.
11. As you drop your tailbone down towards the floor, opening the front of the hips and the pelvic abdomen, lean your head back and gaze upwards at your fingertips.
12. Stretch upwards through your middle back and arms.
13. Hold this pose for five breaths.
14. Inhale and straighten your legs.
15. Lower your arms and bring your legs together again to return to Mountain Pose.
16. Repeat to the other side.

Be Strong. Be Smart. Be Amazing!

Warrior II

Also called "Virabhadrasana II," this pose is meant as a powerful pose to connect our legs to action. Feel the power coursing through your body as you do this pose:

1. Start standing in Mountain Pose.
2. Step or jump your feet wide across the mat.
3. Turn your left foot out by 90 degrees. The heel should be just opposite your right arch.
4. Turn your right foot in slightly.
5. Raise your arms to the sides. Make sure you keep your shoulders down while your palms face the ground.
6. Rest your gaze on the very tips of your left fingers as you extend out through your hands.
7. Exhale and bend your left knee. Your thigh should be parallel to the floor and your knee should be above the ankle.
8. Hold the pose for several seconds, then straighten your legs.

STEP 7: THE IMPORTANCE OF REST

1. Begin by standing on Mountain Pose.
2. Step your feet wide apart. Make sure that your hips are facing to the front and lengthen your body, opening up the front of your hips.
3. Turn your right leg, including your thigh, knee and foot, out by 90 degrees.
4. Turn your left leg in about 15 degrees.
5. Raise your arms to shoulder level with your palms facing down towards the floor.
6. Inhale and extend your spine and body upwards and out through the fingertips.
7. On an exhale, stretch your upper body to the

9. Turn your left foot in and the right foot out and repeat the pose to the other side.

TRIANGLE

Also called "Trikonasana," this is a pose aimed at mobilizing the hips and stretching the torso. It should also open your chest to allow you to breathe deeply:

Be Strong. Be Smart. Be Amazing!

right. Your right hip should still be on the same plane as your shoulders.

8. Place your right hand on your right shin, as far down as you can reach comfortably.

9. If you are more flexible, place your hand on the ground behind your calf. Make sure that your chest is open and your spine is straight.

10. Lengthen your ribs and lift from the edge of your left hip.

11. Raise your left arm towards the ceiling, with your palm facing forward.

12. Gaze at your outstretched hand.

13. Open the chest and turning your belly button slightly upwards. You should feel a twist from your left hip up through the spine.

14. Breathe, increasing the twist on each exhalation. Inhale and allow your body to come to standing.

15. Repeat the pose on the other side.

Balance Pose

Tree

Tree or "Vrksasana" is a pose aimed to perfect the balance and focus of the mind. In this pose, the lower body provides the support for the upper body as the body stands with grace and strength:

1. Stand in Mountain Pose.
2. Shift your weight gradually from your left foot to your right foot and focus your awareness on your feet.
3. With your eyes open, fix your gaze on a point a few feet away from you. It's important to pick a point that is not moving, since gazing at this fixed spot with help you find balance and support you from falling.
4. Shifting your weight slowly onto you right leg, keep it strong as you bring your heel into your right ankle. Left toe is pointed on the floor.

Be Strong. Be Smart. Be Amazing!

5. If you feel safe and comfortable begin to raise your left resting either on your calf with your knee turned outward or on your inner thigh.
6. Make sure your toes are pointing to the floor. You can use your hand to guide your foot if you want.
7. Using your left hand, gently draw your left knee back to help open up your hip.
8. As you perform this step, be conscious of the position of your hips; they should be squared and facing directly in front of you.
9. Lengthen your spine by pointing your tailbone towards the floor and drawing in the pelvic bone.
10. Pull your bellybutton towards your spine and extend your spine by lowering your shoulders as you lengthen the back of your neck.
11. Bring your hands towards your chest and press your palms together.
12. On an inhale, if you are balanced, raise your arms above your head.
13. Open up your chest by squeezing your shoulder blades together.
14. Keep easing your bent knee backward.

STEP 7: THE IMPORTANCE OF REST

15. Keep your gaze fixed and remember to breathe easily.
16. Hold the pose for three (3) breathes.
17. Lower your arms slowly.
18. Rotate your left leg in front of you so that your bent knee points ahead of you.
19. Straighten your bent leg by raising your foot in front of you and then slowly lowering it to the floor.
20. Repeat to the other side.

Now move to the floor for bending and relaxation poses.

BENDING POSES

CAT POSE

Cat Pose or "Bidalasana" is a pose that helps increase flexibility in your spine. When practiced regularly, this pose can help alleviate back pain. It also stretches your neck and helps to stimulate your abdominal organs:

1. Get on your hands and knees on the floor.

Be Strong. Be Smart. Be Amazing!

2. Keep your hands directly beneath your shoulders and your knees directly beneath your hips.
3. Breathe in deeply.
4. On an exhale, gently pull your abdominal muscles backwards and towards your spine.
5. Tuck your tailbone down and under.
6. Gently contract your glutes (bums).
7. Spread your fingers. Your middle finger should be facing forward.
8. Gaze at the floor.
9. Press the middle of your back towards the ceiling. Your spine should be rounded upwards.
10. Curl your head inwards. Look at the floor between your knees. Don't force your chin to your chest.
11. Repeat 10 to 20 times.
12. Release by sitting backwards on your heels with your torso upright.

SEATED FORWARD BEND

Also called "Paschimothanasana," this is a pose that stretches your neck, back,

STEP 7: THE IMPORTANCE OF REST

hamstrings, and calves. It also helps alleviate stress:

1. Sit down on the floor with your legs stretched straight out in front of you.
2. Point your toes towards the ceiling.
3. Stretch your lower back and raise your arms above your head.
4. Look forward.
5. Slowly bend forward.
6. Stretch the crown of your head upwards. Try not to let your lower back cave in; you should be bending at your hips. Don't let your legs move or tilt. Stop when you can't bend further without moving your lower back.
7. Place your hands on your lower legs, ankles, or feet.
8. Lightly pull on them to continue stretching with each exhale.
9. Stretch your arms out forward. Hold for a moment.
10. Then, slowly raise your torso up. Try not to move your legs.
11. Sit up straight.
12. Keep your arms above your head as if they were at the beginning of the pose.

Be Strong. Be Smart. Be Amazing!

CHILD

Also called "Balasana," this is a forward bend as well as a resting or restorative pose. You can perform the child's pose to stretch out your lower back between back bends or as a place to recover during a any practice:

1. Kneel on the floor with your legs together and sit back on your heels.
2. Let your arms hang at your sides.
3. Hinge forward until your chest rests on your thighs and your forehead on the floor. If you need to, you can use your hands to guide yourself forward.
4. Curl your shoulders forward and let your hands extend out stretching through the shoulders. You may also let your hands rest palm up next to your feet.
5. Relax into the pose for five breaths.

STEP 7: THE IMPORTANCE OF REST

MEDITATIVE AND RESTING POSTURE

RESTING POSE

We'll better call this "Rest Pose" instead of "Resting Pose" for now! It's also called "Savasna," and it is typically done at the end of the class as a final relaxation. This pose allows the body time to process information at the end of a class. Even though

Savasana is a resting pose, it's not the same a sleeping! You should stay present and aware during the five to ten minute duration of final relaxation:

1. Lie on your back. Let your feet fall out to either side.
2. Bring your arms alongside your body, but slightly separated from the body, and turn the palms to face upwards.
3. Relax the whole body, including the face.
4. Let your body feel heavy.
5. Let your breath occur naturally.

Be Strong. Be Smart. Be Amazing!

6. To come out, first begin to the deepen the breath.
7. Then move the fingers and toes, awakening the body.
8. Bring the knees into the chest and roll over to one side, keep the eyes closed.
9. Slowly bring yourself back up into a sitting position.

NAMASTE

We'll end with saying "**Namaste**" to each other, which is a sign of respect for another person and a way of saying you recognize the spark of life we each have within us.

Honor the light within yourself and in others. Let it shine bright often and always have an awareness of how your body appreciates different styles of exercise.

STEP 7: THE IMPORTANCE OF REST

Part 5: Hand Outs & Wrap Up

Under the Pillow Affirmation Handout

(Your mom, dad, helper, or instructor should prepare this in advance.)

You'll receive an envelope with a special message on the front and a few (four or five) "positive affirmation" cards inside. These will be unique and specific to *you*. Wait to open your Positive Affirmation Cards until you get home.

You are special and the messages inside are just for you! Read your cards every night before falling asleep and then again when you wake up! This is a great way to end and start the day!

Be Strong. Be Smart. Be Amazing!

Then it's time to relax a bit and discuss any positive feedback from today's session. How did you like the yoga? Do you think you'd like to keep doing yoga and getting **stronger** and more **relaxed** at the same time?

Remember to get enough sleep so you keep yourself feeling fabulous and energized!

HOMEWORK

Do something **relaxing** each night before bed, maybe reading, drawing, looking at your cards, whatever you find helps you wind down. Also track your sleep patterns this week with the **Feeling Faces Worksheet**.

What will you do to relax before bed?

_____
_____
_____
_____
_____
_____
_____

Positive Thoughts ~ The Importance of Rest

"If you continue to tell yourself you are amazing then you will be!"

"We ARE what we think!"

"YOU have the POWER, GIRL!"

"Rest is as important to your body as healthy food and exercise."

Be Strong. Be Smart. Be Amazing!

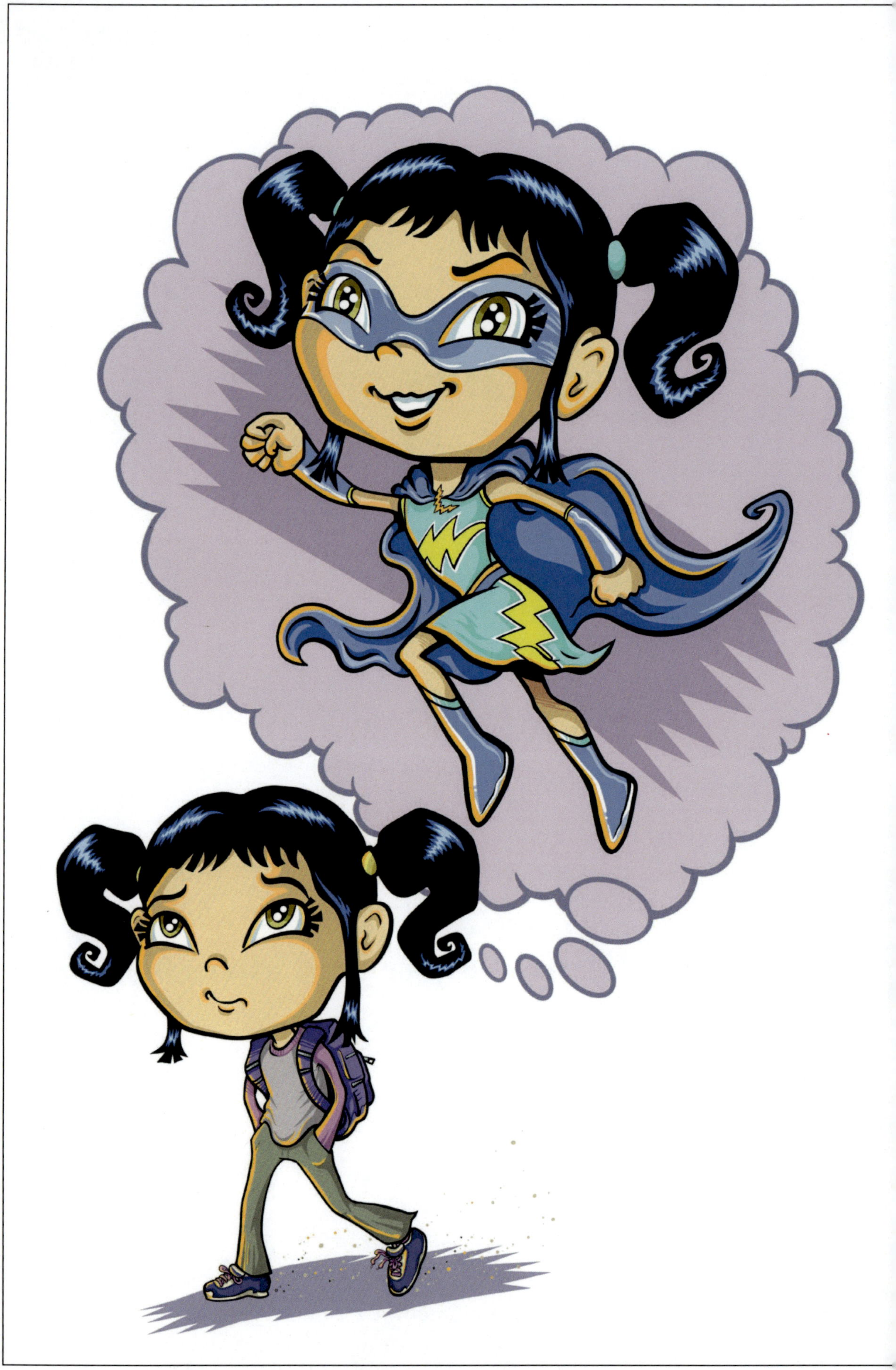

STEP 8: REVIEW AND GRADUATION

Your Final Step and a Whole New Beginning!

Part 1: Kick Off your Final Class

Get Moving!

WARM UP with **stretching**, **jumping jacks**, **running in place** or **laps around the room**, then more **stretching**! Do this for three to five minutes to warm up and burn some excited energy!

Now review last week's homework as well as previous classes, and write your thoughts on the following questions:

What did you like the most about your Girl Power classes?

_____
_____
_____
_____
_____
_____
_____

What will you take with you in the future?

_____
_____

STEP 8: REVIEW AND GRADUATION

_____

_____

_____

_____

_____

Share your thoughts and feelings about the classes.

Overall, what was your favorite class? Why?

_____

_____

_____

What fitness activity did you like best—kickboxing, yoga, boot camp, another?

_____

_____

_____

_____

_____

_____

_____

Be Strong. Be Smart. Be Amazing!

Part 2: Activity

Self-Portrait

Name:_____   Date:_____

Draw a picture of yourself ☺

STEP 8: REVIEW AND GRADUATION

Once you have drawn this latest picture of yourself, compare it to the drawing of yourself you did in the **very first class**.

What is **different**?

Did you draw yourself very small in week one and very large in the last portrait?

Compare any backgrounds or added features in the picture.

Was the first portrait done with a straight smile and this portrait done with a **big smile**?

Write down how you think this second picture is different:

_____

_____

_____

_____

_____

Share your pictures now, if you would like. You may take your portraits **home** or leave them with who has helped you, whatever you would like.

And of course, pick up the supplies as you are finished.

Be Strong. Be Smart. Be Amazing!

Part 3: Freestyle Fitness

Mini Boot Camp

Set up the following:

- One station with jump ropes,
- One with a cone zigzag course, and
- One with hula hoops.

Choose which course you would like to use first, and then enjoy five to ten minutes of "**freestyle fitness**," meaning you can do whatever activity you would like. Also do some kickboxing, running drills, or other work if you have time at the end of class.

I Am Statements

Do "I am statements" while you are at these stations and exercising. Come up with your own "I am statements" and do many of them!

"I am _____!"

"I am _____!"

"I am _____!"

"I am _____!"

"I am _____!"

STEP 8: REVIEW AND GRADUATION

Part 4: Graduation and Wrap Up

This class is a **celebration** of what you have learned and how you view yourself— **strong**, **smart**, **amazing**!

Time for some positive feedback from the class or whoever is helping you.

Review all that you have learned and how far you have come!

Express what the experience gave you and read the **Graduation Letter** on the next page from Mrs. Mahoney.

Be Strong. Be Smart. Be Amazing!

To My Girl Power Girls!

Continue to do the work that you have begun here. You are perfect just as you are. I am forever changed because I have had the pleasure of working with you. I hope that you have enjoyed this experience, even half as much as I have.

Go after whatever you want in this life, I believe you will achieve great things.

Be Strong, Be Smart, Be Amazing!

Mrs. Mahoney

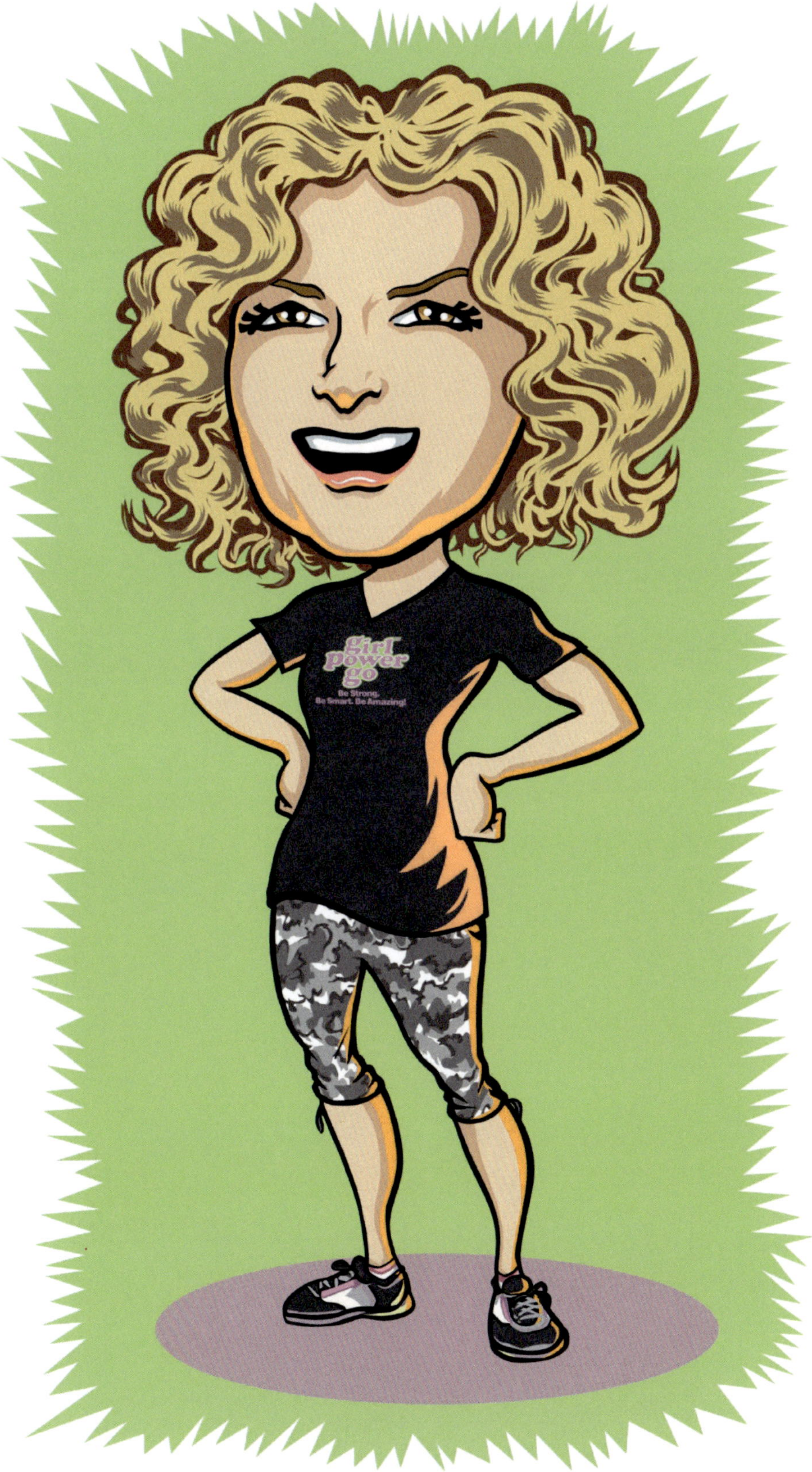
girl power go
Be Strong.
Be Smart. Be Amazing!

Remember!

☙

"Do one thing every day that makes you happy!"

"Be brave and courageous!"

Be kind and caring!"

"Know that you have the POWER to impact others in a positive way!"

"You have one body, take care of it!"

"Your body is changing, but it is just as it should be right now. Love every stage!"

Final Positive Thoughts

For the Week and Beyond!

"You are AMAZING just the way you are!"

"Your body will do ANYTHING you set your mind to!"

"Think it, Believe it, Achieve it!"

"We ARE what we think."

"Nothing worth having is achieved without hard work and determination."

GRADUATION CERTIFICATE!

Get excited! You have worked hard and come so far, and I am so very proud of you! I hope that you now know the **Girl Power** you have within you, and that you keep that for the rest of your life while helping other girls find their **Girl Power**!

Once the person helping you presents you with your **GRADUATION CERTIFICATE**, read it over. Once home, place it somewhere special, and feel free to show it to anyone you like, telling them all about your **Girl Power**.

Girl Power

Certificate of Graduation

has successfully completed the 8-week Girl Power Program

offered by Girl Power Go, LLC.

Take all that you have learned

and be the BEST you that you can be!

Think it – Believe it – Achieve it

You have the POWER to do great things!

_____   __/__/__
Signature of Instructor   Date

Approved by

Erin C. Mahoney

Creator of Girl Power

This page left blank so you can cut out the graduation certificate on the previous page!

"Somebody who has had Girl Power is strong."

A letter from Girl Power "Gaby" Gabrielle!

I'M 14 NOW, but when I was seven or eight, there was a girl on my school bus and she would always sit behind me. (I would always sit somewhat towards the front of the bus—not the back because that's where all the older kids were.) She would always end up saying names to me or she would say some really mean things (she called me a tom-boy) and I really didn't know what to do, I was quite confused. It was a first time for me, so I would just kind of let it happen—I really didn't know what to do.

I talked about it with my mom and she told me, "Oh, you've got to stand up for yourself, you have to tell her to back off!" I was really scared because I was really shy back then. I was telling my aunt about it, and she was telling me what to do—all of this stuff totally different from what my mom said, all of these additional ideas.

My aunt Erin found me a shirt that said, I am not a tom-boy, I'm an athlete, and I started wearing it on the bus. The older girls didn't know what to do—they left me alone after that. So Aunt Erin had this idea to teach other girls about this, so they wouldn't get into the situation I was, and they would know what to do.

I can remember the first class—it was in my Girl Scout troop, actually. My aunt came to my friend's house and she gave a presentation about what we need to do if girls are picking on us, or boys, or anyone at all. How would we need to deal with it? We called it "Girl Power."

Next, my aunt brought it to my school, Elmwood School in Hopkinton, where I went for elementary school. I remember going to Girl Power classes there. The girl who was picking on me was in the class, so it was kind of awkward. But as I was thinking she was the person who was doing it to me, I realized maybe she's doing it because she's getting picked on as well, or something's happening on her side that is causing her to do this stuff to me.

The Girl Power class was really fun. I can remember I became friends with her—the girl who was picking on me. We're kind of friends now, we talk a little bit. She has gotten better. She doesn't say anything mean to me anymore.

There was this one drill where we had to give each person a compliment and then give another person a different one. She would always come up to me and say the exact same one: "You look great today!" So in the end it was so much fun and I loved it because now we're good friends. It was really fun.

We came up with new t-shirts. They said "Girl Power" on them, and it was a girl standing, wearing a cape. Whenever I look at it I think, "That's a strong person." I always imagine somebody strong—and somebody who has had Girl Power is strong.

Lots of girls at Elmwood, which is a school for second and third graders, did the Girl Power class, and they opened it up to kids of other ages, too, 4th and 5th, and I think some first-graders.

I definitely was shy when I was younger but not anymore. Girl Power is definitely part of why I am not shy anymore. In every Girl Power class we had, Aunt Erin would have us get in front of the class and say something we believe about ourselves. One thing I said was, "I'm a strong person." Hearing myself say that really kind of broke me out of my shell. It made me think what I was saying was true about myself.

I know other girls who went through Girl Power. I have a friend who had a lot of problems with her weight and after she did the program with my aunt she had a different perspective of herself. Now she totally thinks of herself as not being overweight, and not being judged inside other people's heads, like what they think about her isn't important.

I'm in high school now, so it's not really a big problem, but in middle school I can remember, I played on the eighth grade soccer team and there were these girls on my team. They would kind of tease me about certain stuff. I didn't really appreciate it, obviously, and no one would stick up for me and I didn't see anybody tell them to back off or anything, so I kind of had to stand up for myself and I confronted them about it, and all I could think about was my aunt in the back of my head telling me, "You can do this! Don't be scared."

I told them, "I don't appreciate you doing what you're doing to me and I need you to stop now."

"Oh, yeah, I didn't know it was bothering you, I'm sorry," they said. It was that easy. Maybe people just need to stand up once in a while.

I definitely think other girls should do Girl Power. I think the best time is about third grade, about the age I was. When girls start early they're carrying it through their lives—like their entire life they're going to use it. It's just a powerful tool.

I'm really proud of my aunt for taking this next step with Girl Power (this book). She's just the best person ever. She's like a second mom to me. If she heard that it would definitely make her cry. Thank you so much! I definitely think other girls should do Girl Power too.

—GABRIELLE

About Mrs. Erin

ERIN C. MAHONEY has over 29 years of experience in the health and fitness industry. After serving in the United States Air Force as a medic, Erin found a way to combine her healthcare background with her passion for fitness. She has been a certified personal trainer and certified group fitness instructor since 2001. She has held specialized certifications in yoga and kickboxing. Erin studied meditation, relaxation and stress reduction at the Center of Mindfulness at the University of Massachusetts Medical Center. Most recently Erin has moved into EFT (Emotional Freedom Technique) work in the form of Tapping.

Erin is the founder and creator of Girl Power Go which is an empowerment program for girls. This program was specifically designed to get girls ages 7 to 14 excited about being strong, self-confident, independent, and healthy. Erin saw a need for this important and relevant program and created unique four, six, and eight-week programs that give girls the tools they need to make good decisions in our ever demanding society. Erin combines life skills, fitness, positive thinking, creativity and fun into her program which reinforces her message to each girl that they can *Be Strong, Be Smart, Be Amazing!* Girl Power has been running successfully in many communities in her home state of Massachusetts. Erin has written this book in an effort to bring this program to the world! The demand for this program continues to grow and plans are in place to expand so that Erin and her Girl Power Go team might empower thousands of girls across the globe!

Erin incorporated her health and wellness company under the name of B3 Training, Inc. (Now called Girl Power Go), and with this, Erin has been able to expand and offer many programs. Girl Power Go offers a full range of services in the fitness field. Everything from group and one-on-one personal training, novice and marathon training running programs, and kids empowerment programs. Energy work and adult empowerment programs have been added as well as business and personal motivational coaching. Girl Power Go has also joined forces with the Girl Scouts of Central and Western Massachusetts as a Community Partner. They love the message that the Girl Power Go program teaches, and Erin has created customized programs that give Daisies, Brownies, Juniors and Cadets the tools and experiences they need to develop leadership qualities through the key skills integral to Girl Scouting. Erin hopes to work with Girl Scouts all over the nation in the future.

Kid Power is an enrichment program created for boys and girls teaching them leadership, respect, and strength. This program works with kids during their school day to inspire them and help them build the foundation to make good decisions well beyond the classroom.

Erin is a seasoned running coach who has trained both novice and marathon runners. Having completed seven marathons herself, she is passionate about the sport. Serving on the Board of Directors for the Hopkinton Running Club as the Director of Training, Erin was instrumental in creating one of its most successful programs. In its first year, her "Couch to 5k" program successfully took over 60 non-runners and transformed them into runners. Now in its fourth year, Erin has grown this program to neighboring towns and has helped hundreds of runners reach their goals. Erin inspires her runners to *Be Courageous, Be Consistent, Be Committed.*

Erin lives in Milford, Massachusetts with her husband and two sons. She is passionate about what she does and takes pride in creating all of these programs that inspire and motivate people to uncover the power that they have within themselves. Her philosophy is that people have the ability to achieve any and all things that they set their minds to. It's her goal to help them get there!

This page left blank so you can cut out the cards on the next page!

APPENDIX: AFFIRMATION CARDS

It's important to make these fun and beautiful, to capture the girls' interest and create value, and to have fun with it!

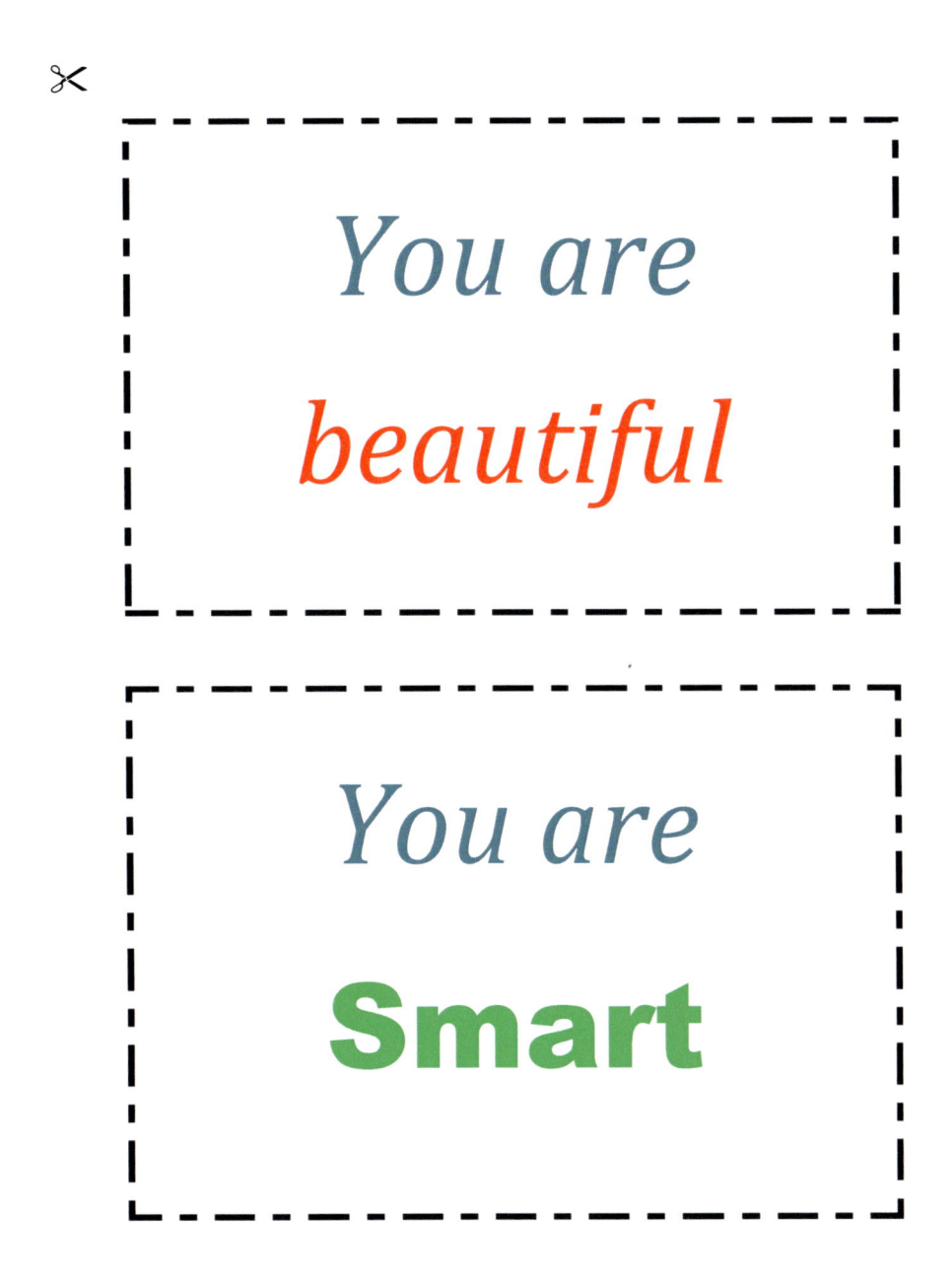

✂

You are beautiful

You are **Smart**

This page left blank so you can cut out the cards on the previous page!

You are
CreaTive

You are
a good friend

You have a great
sense of humor

This page left blank so you can cut out

the cards on the previous page!

You have a great
SMILE

You are
a strong leader

This page left blank so you can cut out the cards on the previous page!

You are

Kind

You are

Amazing

This page left blank so you can cut out

the cards on the previous page!

You are Powerful

*You are **FABULOUS***

This page left blank so you can cut out
the cards on the previous page!

You have *great energy!*

You are caring & considerate

This page left blank so you can cut out
the cards on the previous page!

You have the POWER to make it a great day!

Do your best.

Your best is

***always** good enough!*

This page left blank so you can cut out the cards on the previous page!

You have a great
attitude

You are

funny

You are

A good **sport**

This page left blank so you can cut out
the cards on the previous page!

You are
thoughtful

You are
perfect just the way you are

This page left blank so you can cut out the cards on the previous page!

Appendix: Bracelets and Beads

In the beginning of Girl Power I created and did an AMAZING project with them. We created Girl Power bracelets and I talked them through what this bracelet meant and would represent to/for them. I have attached the document I would give them with this activity. Pretty powerful stuff!

I discontinued this piece of the program because it was too expensive to maintain but it's certainly something that they could do within the workbook on their own or be added back into Girl Power classes in some cases. It's so meaningful!

What The Beads Mean and Defining Who You Want To Be

1. The "You" bead is your birthstone and the first bead we select.

2. Then you choose the "primary stones" which represent the people you surround yourself with: your parents, siblings, close friends—the people that love and support you.

3. Next we take a look at the "personality and quality" beads. These are the beads that make you <u>YOU</u> or who you WANT to become:
   - Confident – Silver
   - Faith – Pearl
   - Girl Power – Rainbow Pink
   - Friendship& Friend – Dark Purple/Blue Rainbow
   - Honest & Trustworthy – Charcoal Gray
   - Helpful & Wise – Light Purple/Pink Rainbow
   - Nature Lover – Green

4. Charm Selection – Your bracelet will be closed off with a high quality sterling silver clasp and a charm of your choice. You will choose from the following charms:
   - Faith
   - Hope
   - Love
   - Peace
   - Joy

Photo Album

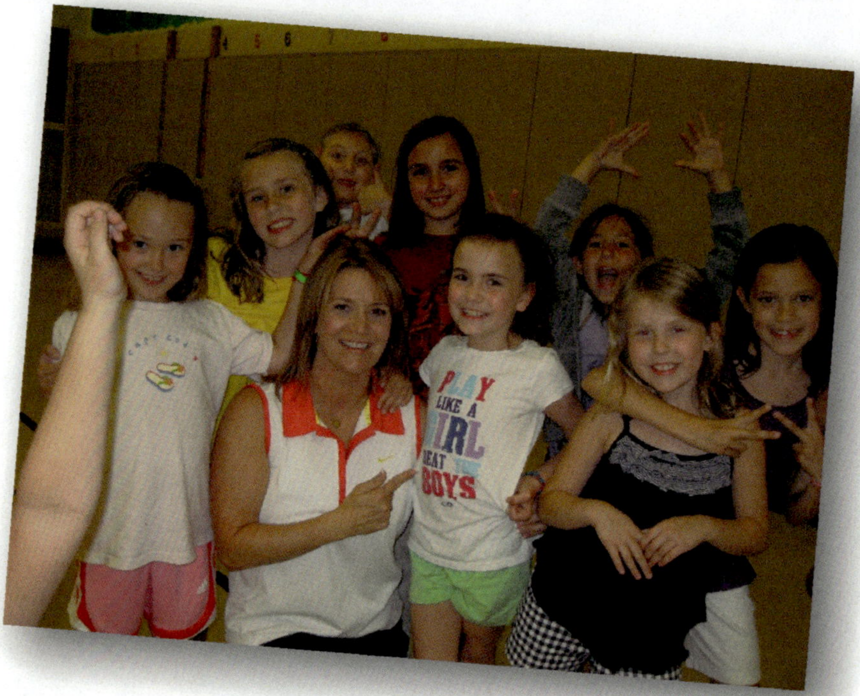
PLAY
LIKE A
BOYS

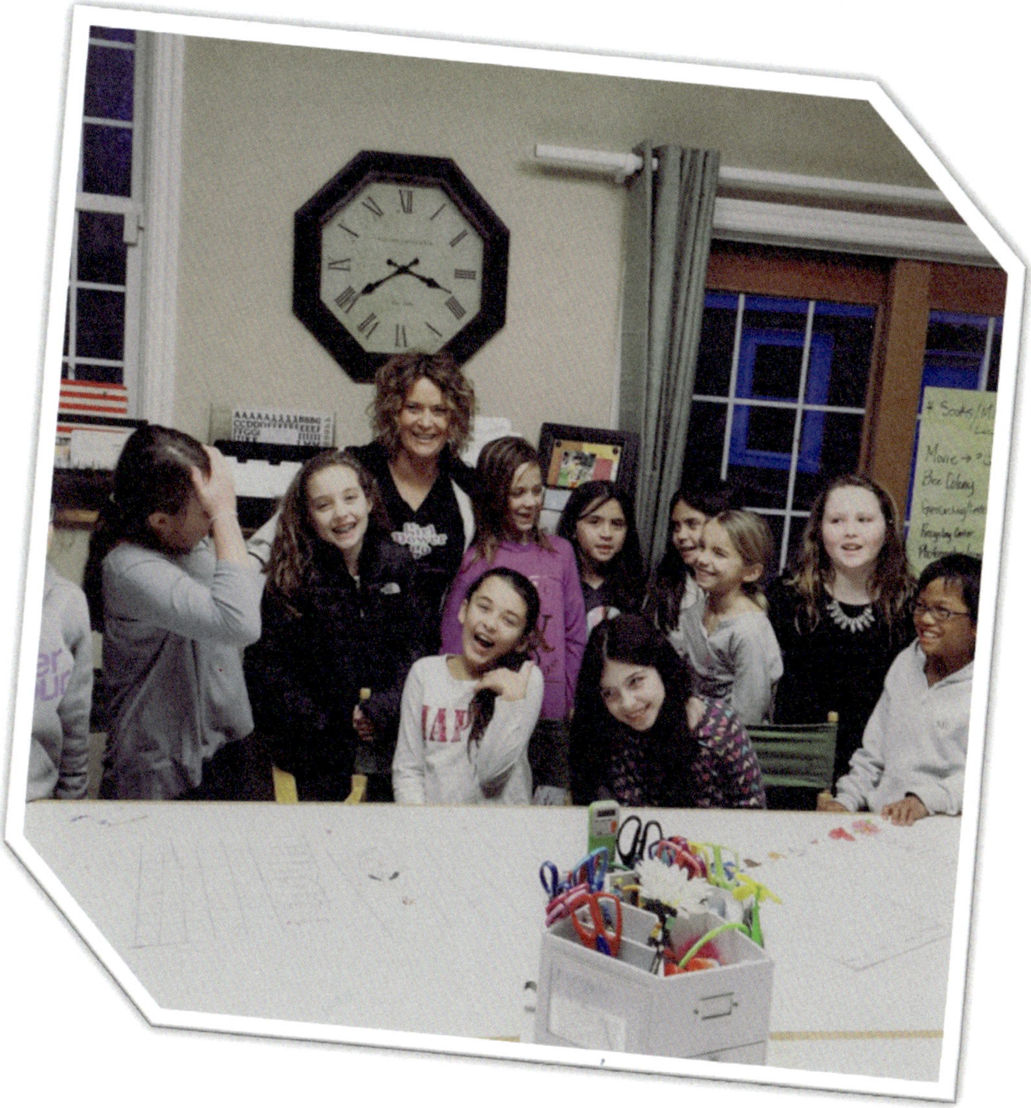

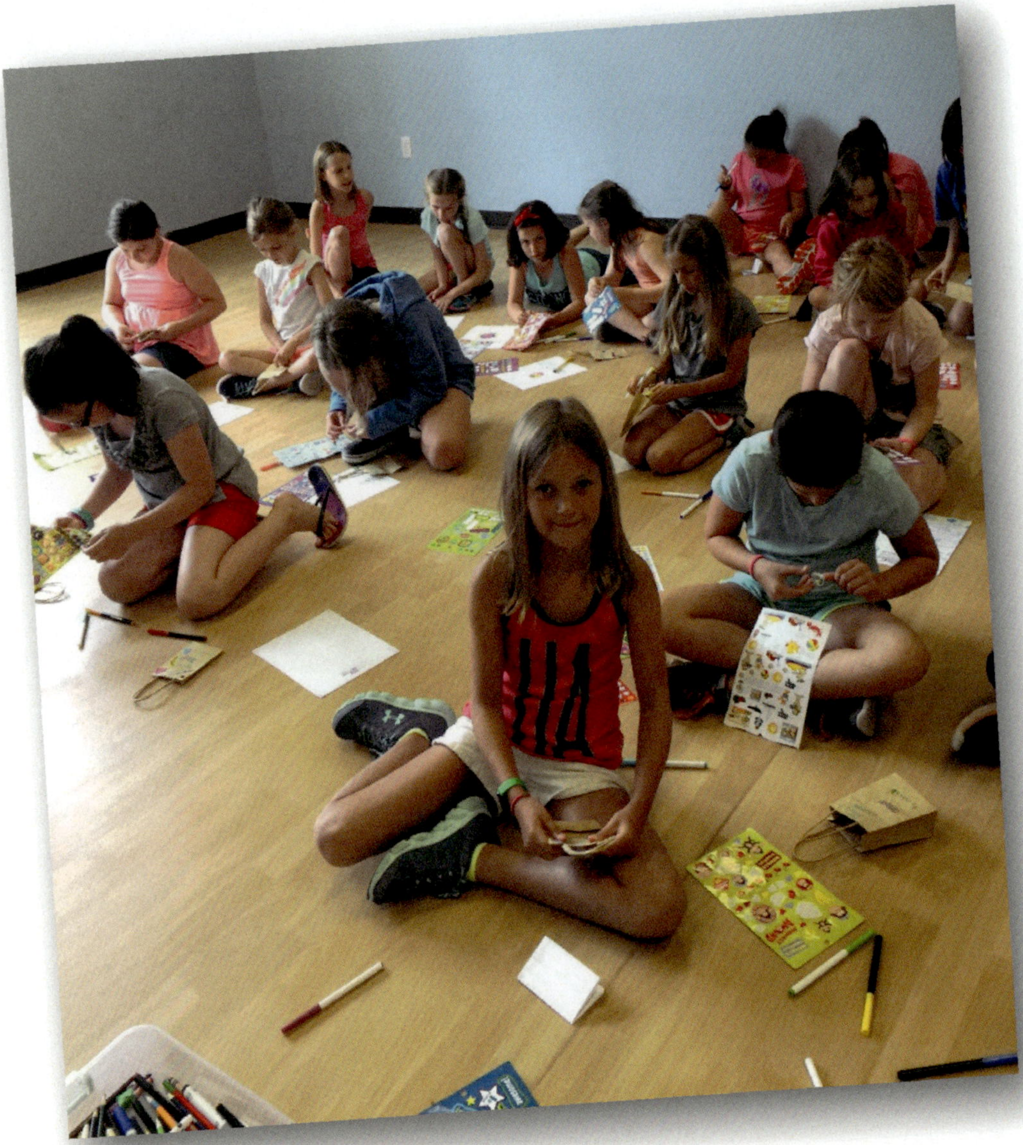

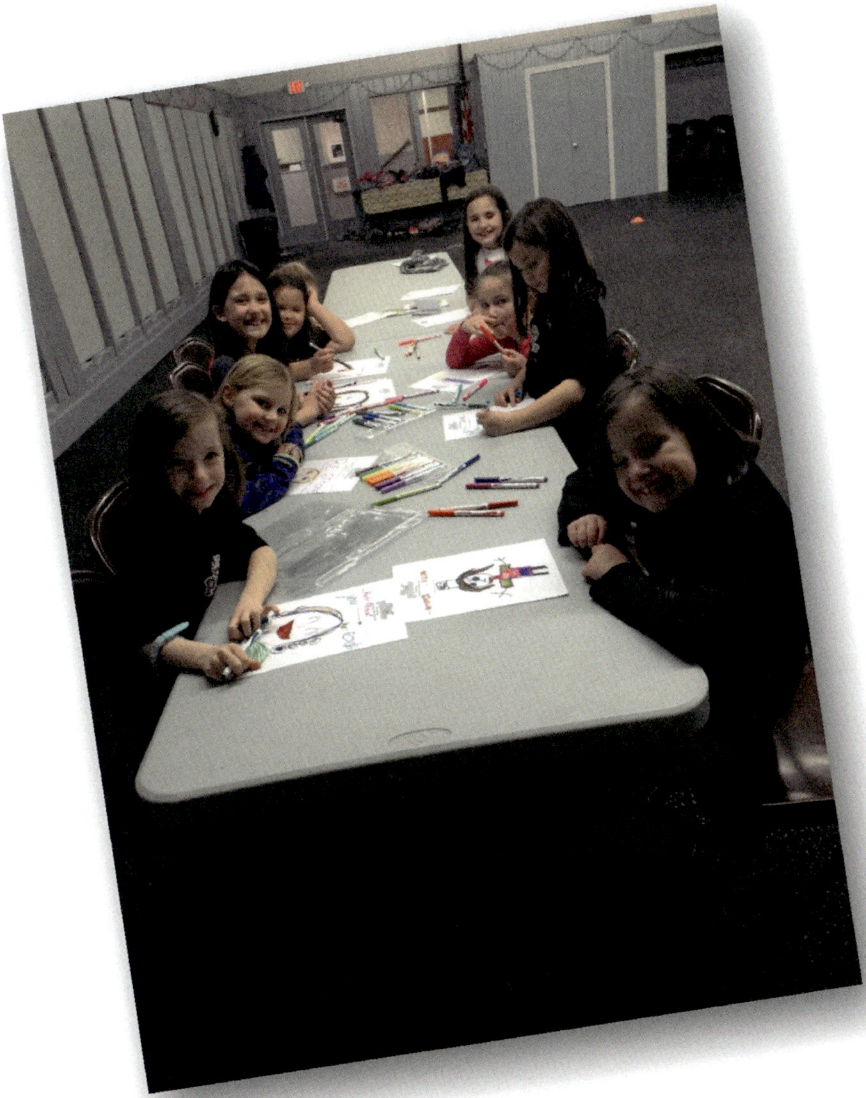

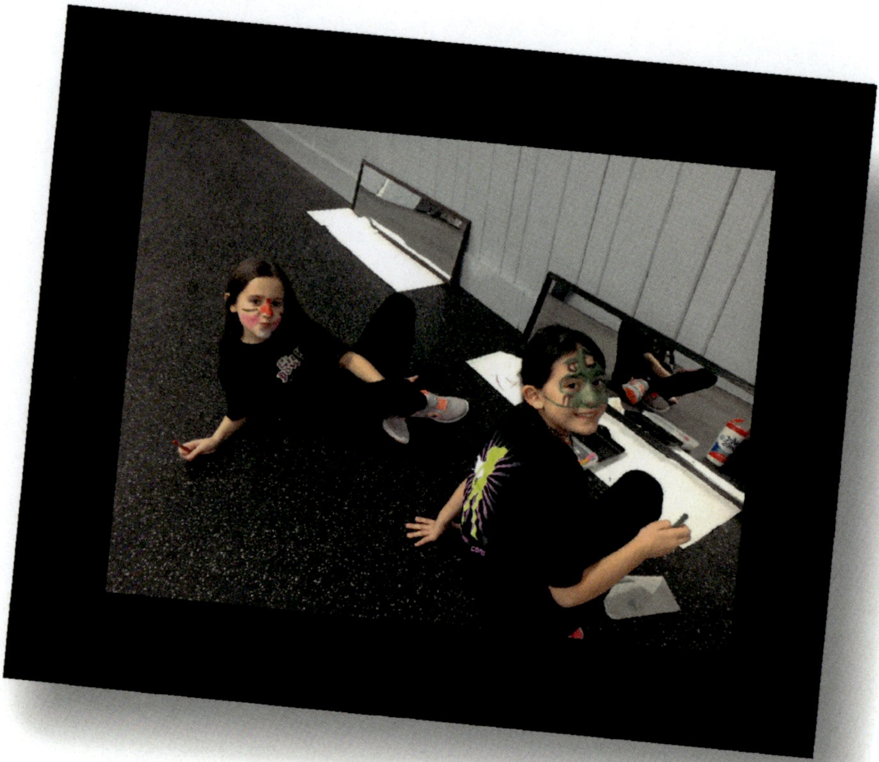

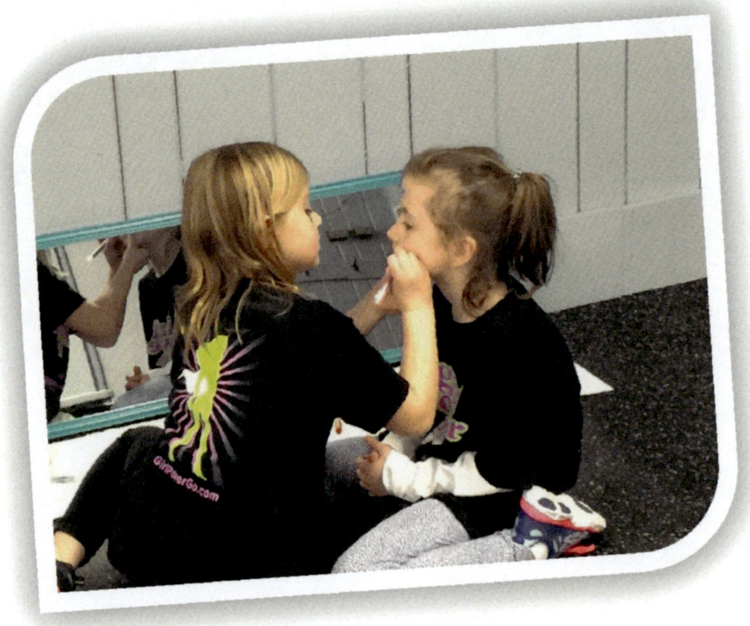
GirlPowerGo.com

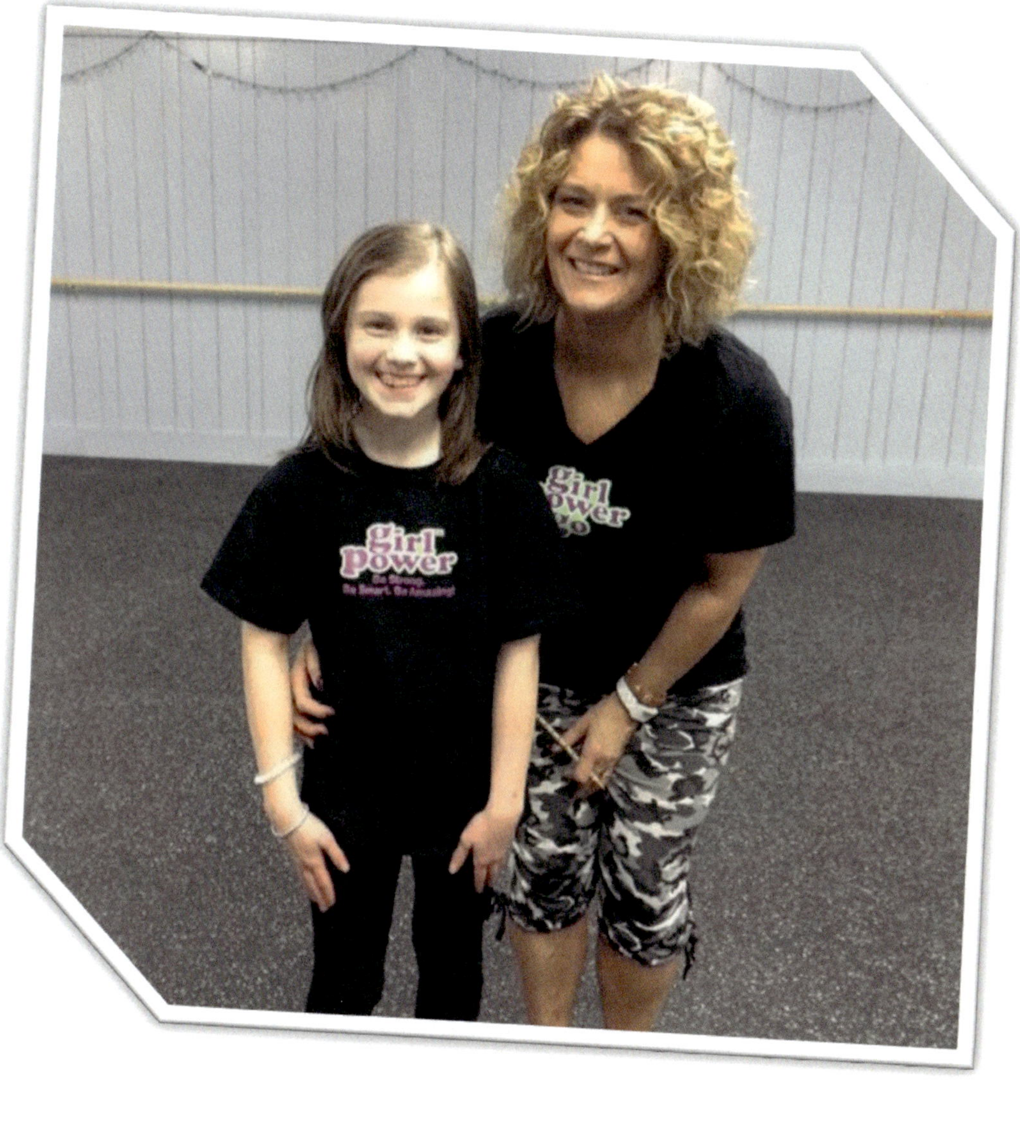
girl
power

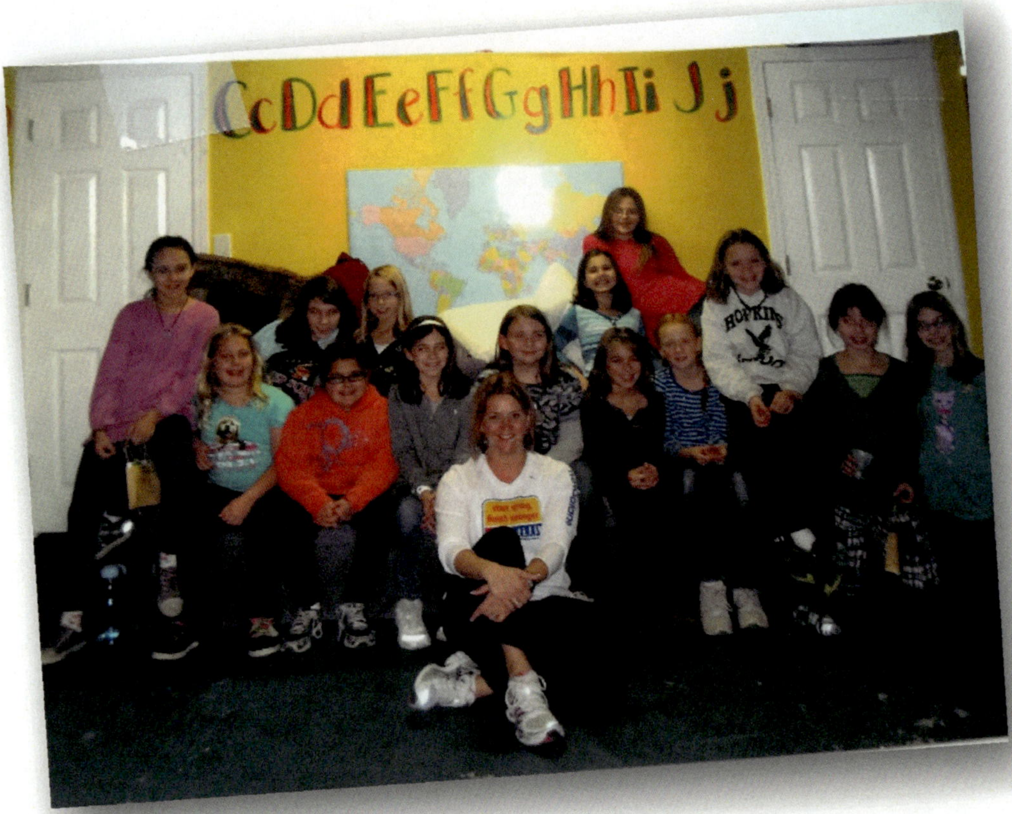
Cc Dd Ee Ff Gg Hh Ii Jj

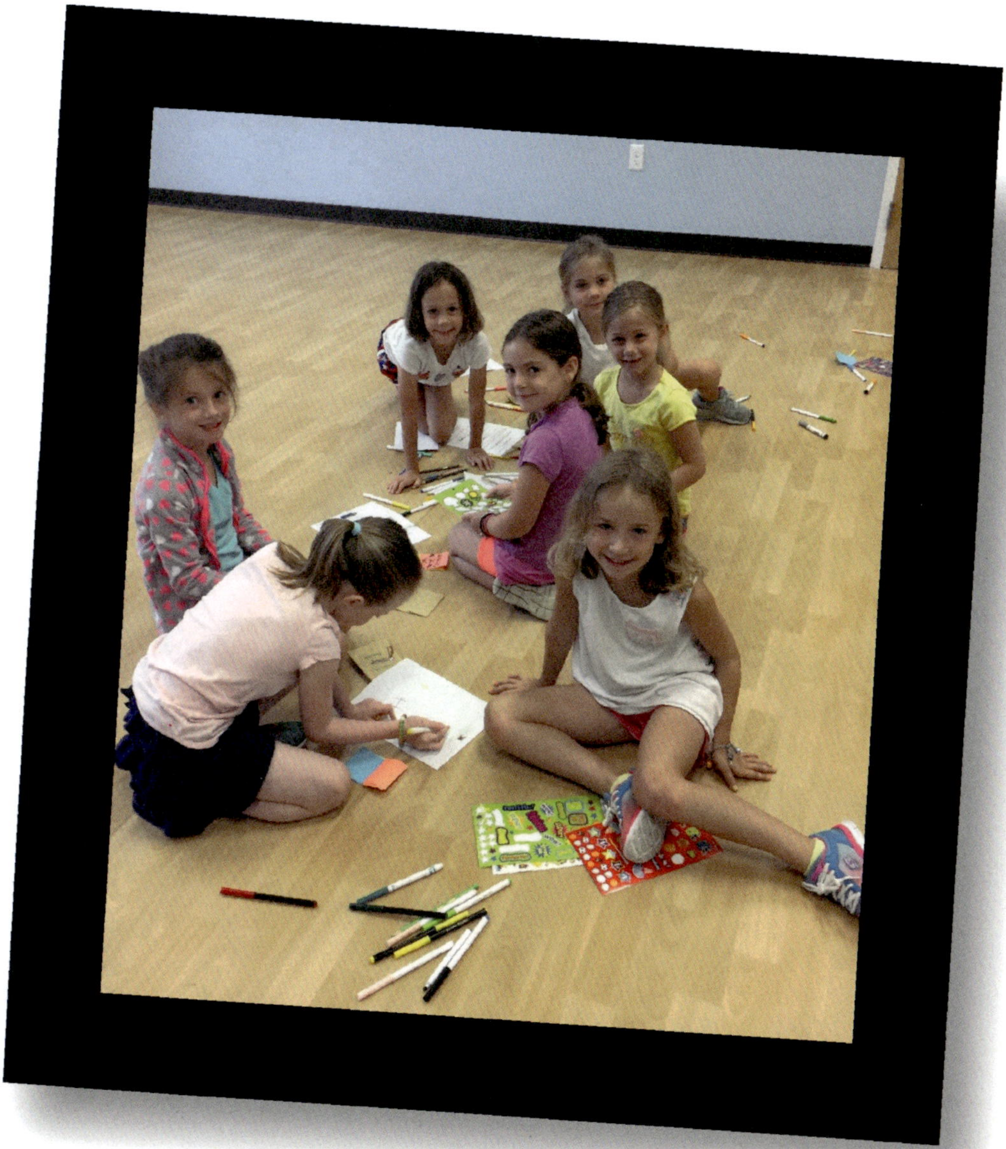

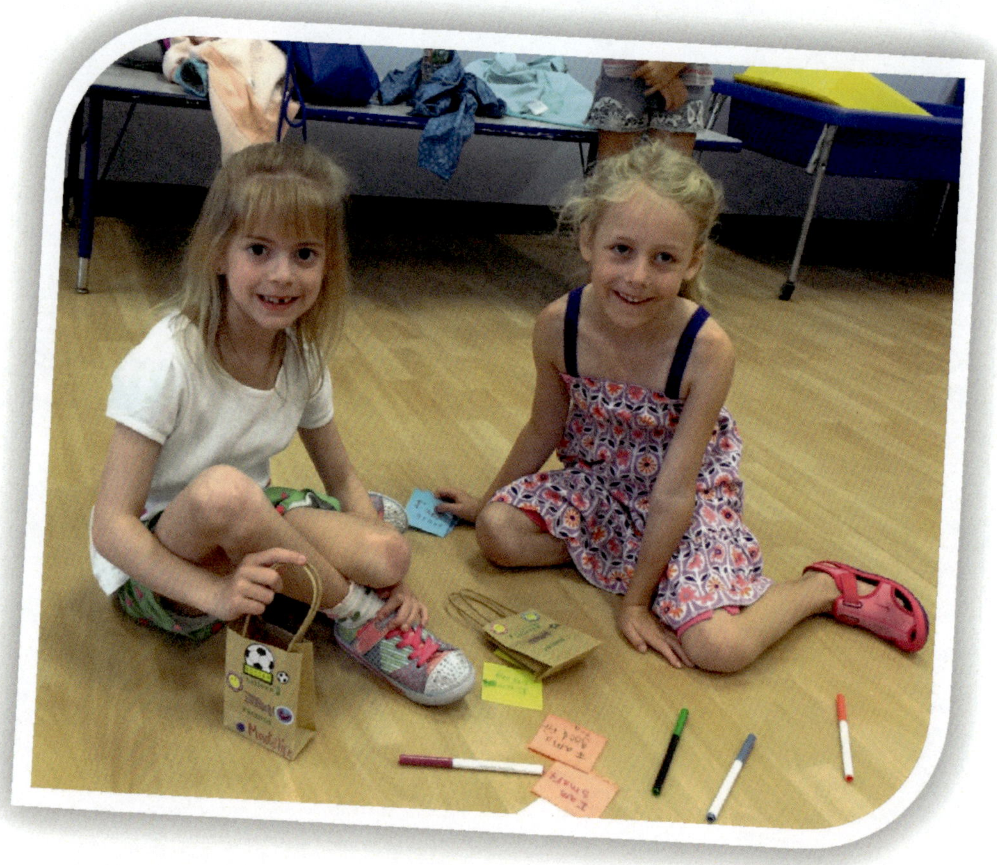

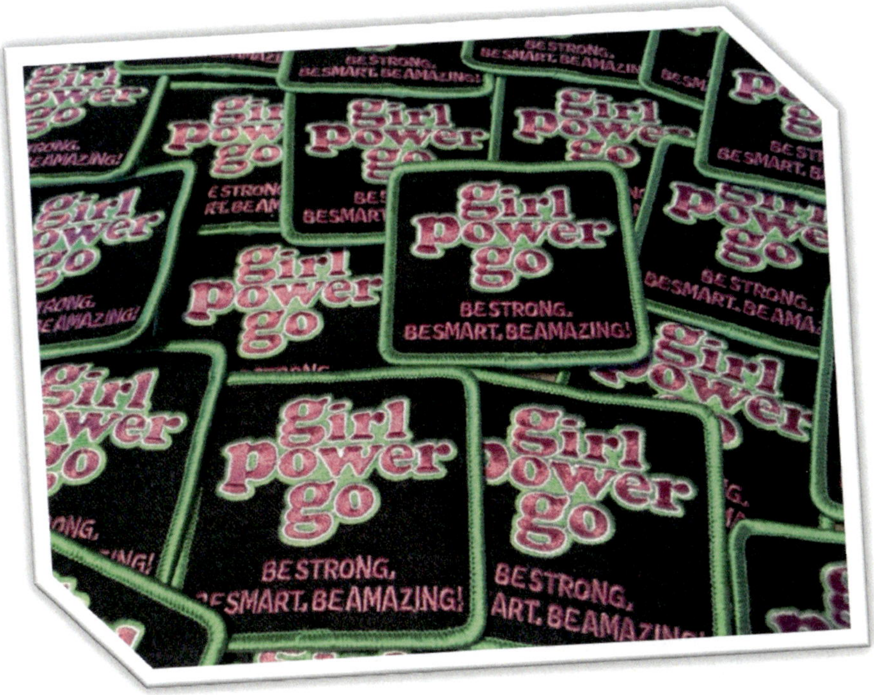
girl
power
go
BE STRONG,
BE SMART, BE AMAZING!

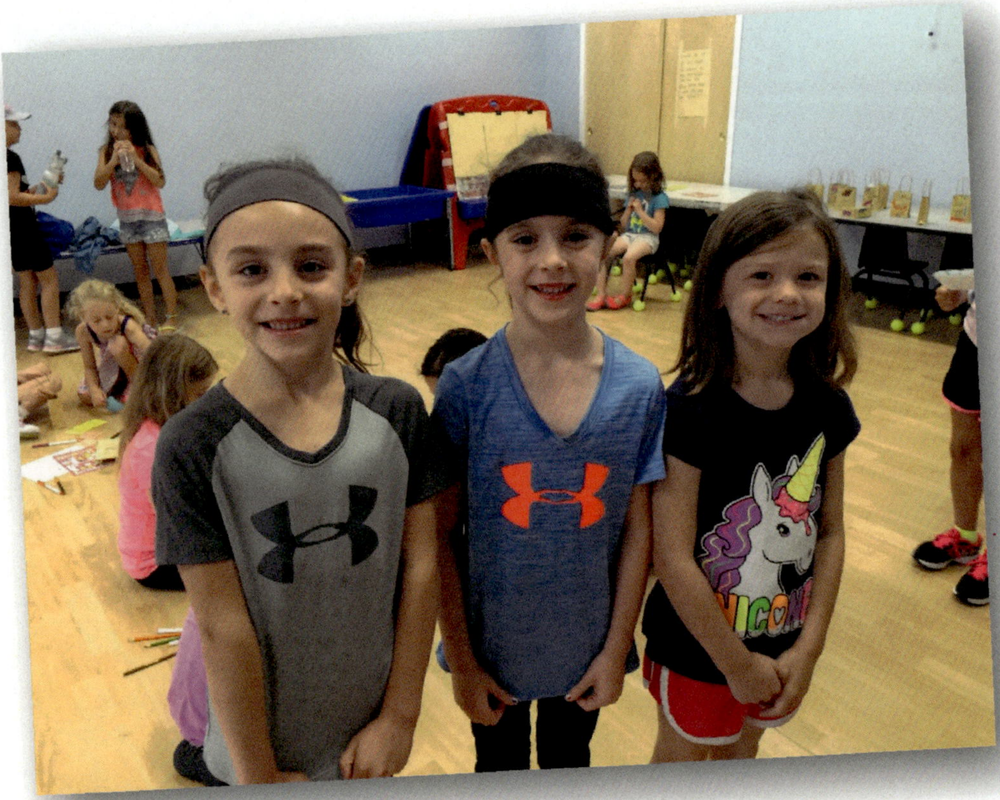

PLACE YOUR CLASS PHOTOS AND DRAWINGS ON THESE PAGES!

Testimonials

"GIRL POWER GO is an amazing program that has had such a profound and positive impact on our daughter's life. She is 8 years old and suffers from Generalized Anxiety Disorder, Social Anxiety Disorder, Sensory Processing Disorder and possible Selective Mutism. At home, she is outgoing, loud and active. However, school and social situations are extremely stressful for her and she often becomes paralyzed and unable to speak. It's as if she lives a double life. The beautiful, smart, strong and hilarious child we know at home struggles so much to get through everyday life and ordinary social situations. It is heartbreaking to see.

Recently, her 3rd grade teacher reported that she is gradually becoming able to participate in class, specifically during the morning meeting time when students are required to greet their classmates in a loud, clear voice. In the past, she would cry and hide her face. She eventually started to wave to the other students instead of hiding, and most recently has been able to vocalize her greeting to them and her teachers. Last week she even participated in an activity that required her to share something about herself. This might not seem like a big deal for most children, but for her it was a huge milestone.

Girl Power Go has been instrumental in helping her to gain confidence and to find her voice. Thank you from the bottom of my heart for helping her to recognize the strength, power and courage that we always knew was inside of her.

— S.C. AND K.C FROM MASSACHUSETTS

"Girl Power will last a lifetime with any girl who goes through the program. It will last with the parents as well, because what goes on are great opportunities for discussions between a parent and a girl."

—SHERENE, MASTER'S DEGREE IN EDUCATIONAL PSYCHOLOGY

"Thanks once again for a wonderful evening with our girls. They simply love you. We talked about what they learned and they talked on and on. You are doing really important work: motivator, role model, friend, teacher. We are blessed to have you in our girls' lives."

—ANNE C., RN BC MSN ANP, NURSE EDUCATOR

"Thanks Auntie for loving me enough to start this great program!"

—GABY, GIRL POWER STUDENT

"I really liked the class and want to go again. It made me feel strong, proud, awesome and undefeated! Thank you Miss Erin, you're the best teacher EVER!!!"

—ALINA, GIRL POWER STUDENT

"My daughter had a fantastic experience. Girl Power is all about promoting healthy minds and bodies in girls by learning great exercises, healthy eating habits, empowerment messages, etc. Erin is full of positive energy, enthusiasm and fun, which is contagious! The girls leave every class rejuvenated and excited. My daughter still talks about her wonderful experience in Girl Power!"

—Ashley, Girl Power Mom

"Girl Power helped my daughter appreciate the 'girl' inside. She now realizes that she is not a tomboy but an AMAZING girl athlete! Thank you Erin for giving so much of yourself to help our strong, smart and AMAZING girls!"

—Michelle, Girl Power Mom

"Thank you Erin for offering such a valuable class to our girls!"

—Taleen, Girl Power Mom

"Thank you for being part of our troop's success!"
—Lee Burns, Leader to Hopkinton Girl Scout Troop 72975

"The Girl Power Program is a wonderful inspiration program for girls, teenagers and young women. I have been a Girl Power Instructor for three years and I am honored to be part of it! This program focuses on teaching with a loving heart many life fundamentals such as how to be a good friend, how to be independent and how to make healthy choices. A few of the foundational principles being taught include honesty, trustworthiness, and respect for oneself and others. There are many different activities in the program that are designed to build self-esteem and confidence including arts and crafts, physical fitness, games, and motivational encouragement. The program also helps the students develop useful tools like healthy eating charts and sleep preparation guidelines.

"I have seen first-hand how this program can motivate and transform the girls into fearless warriors. Often new participants come into the program feeling shy, quiet and unsure. But gradually the principles covered in the program help empower the students to build new relationships and transform them into confident and powerful girls. Witnessing the students learn and grow is very exciting to see and I am always grateful to help facilitate this change as a Girl Power Instructor!"

—A‍nn M, Girl Power, Yoga, and Spinning Instructor and Healing Practitioner

"Girl power brings such a positive energy and focus on loving yourself from the inside out. It reinforces to young girls to be confident, strong, and that true beauty comes from a kind soul. It's an empowering, beautiful experience that I'm happy my daughter had the opportunity to participate in!"

—Caitlin Theodorou, Girl Power Mom

"I was introduced to Erin Mahoney's Girl Power program three years ago when she spoke for the first time to my daughter's Girl Scout troop. The powerful, enthusiastic, and positive messages she has given these girls will guide them as they continue to grow into strong confident young ladies. It has been a pleasure working with Erin as she tailors these messages to fit the needs each year for my group. Erin lives her life as an example for all girls."

—Meghan Kirby, Girl Scout Leader and Girl Power Mom

"It's fun. I love her activities. The Name Game and the Healthy Eating Food Challenge are my favorites!"

—Leah, Age 9, Girl Power Student

"Hats off to Erin Mahoney for creating a positively enriching and empowering program for young girls! When my daughter was in 1st grade she participated in Girl Power. Now in 3rd grade she still talks about her experience! Some of her favorite memories were the Brave and Courageous class when she painted warrior paint on her face. Not only was it a fun and silly class but she also took home the valuable life lesson that she has the power to be the best that she can be, always! She also loved doing yoga and learning new poses. Her favorite part was at the end when Erin gave her an envelope with colorful printed-out characteristics specifically picked for her. My daughter still has those characteristics hanging on her wall to read every day. As a mother of a young girl I can't think of a better way for my daughter to spend her time after school. Erin Mahoney is a true blessing with an energy so positive you can feel it seep into your soul."

—Yvonne Frohn, Girl Power Mom

"I was lucky enough to be introduced to Girl Power two years ago. After attending one of the Girl Power classes, I knew this was something I needed to be involved in! The energy of every lesson Erin created is well thought-out and extremely effective. The activities and messages are well received by the girls all while having an amazing time! I believe with all that is expected from our girls today, Girl Power reinforces how important it is for them to believe in themselves!"

—Moreen Hardcastle, Girl Power Mom and Girl Power Instructor.

"After Part 1, the girls were so enthusiastic about Girl Power that they couldn't wait for Part 2. They happily talked amongst themselves about the program and then shared their well thought out feedback with Kristine and I. It was impressive how well they internalized the ideas that Erin was trying to impress upon them. I think they grasped and retained the information because of the way it was presented to them. Erin made learning fun! The affirmations the girls exclaimed gave me goose bumps: "I am strong! I am smart! I am pretty! I am amazing!" The girls earned a "My Best Self" badge and a "Girl Power" fun badge. They also gained a beneficial dose of self-esteem and empowerment. Bottom line—I loved this program and will be calling on Erin again in the future. I highly recommend Girl Power. I can't say enough about it."

—Maria B.
Girl Scout Brownie Troop 30851 Co-Leader and Mom of Two VERY Strong, Smart, Amazing Girls

WRITE YOUR OWN TESTIMONIAL HERE ON THESE PAGES!

What did you like the best about Girl Power?

What has Girl Power helped you to accomplish?

What do you now believe about yourself?

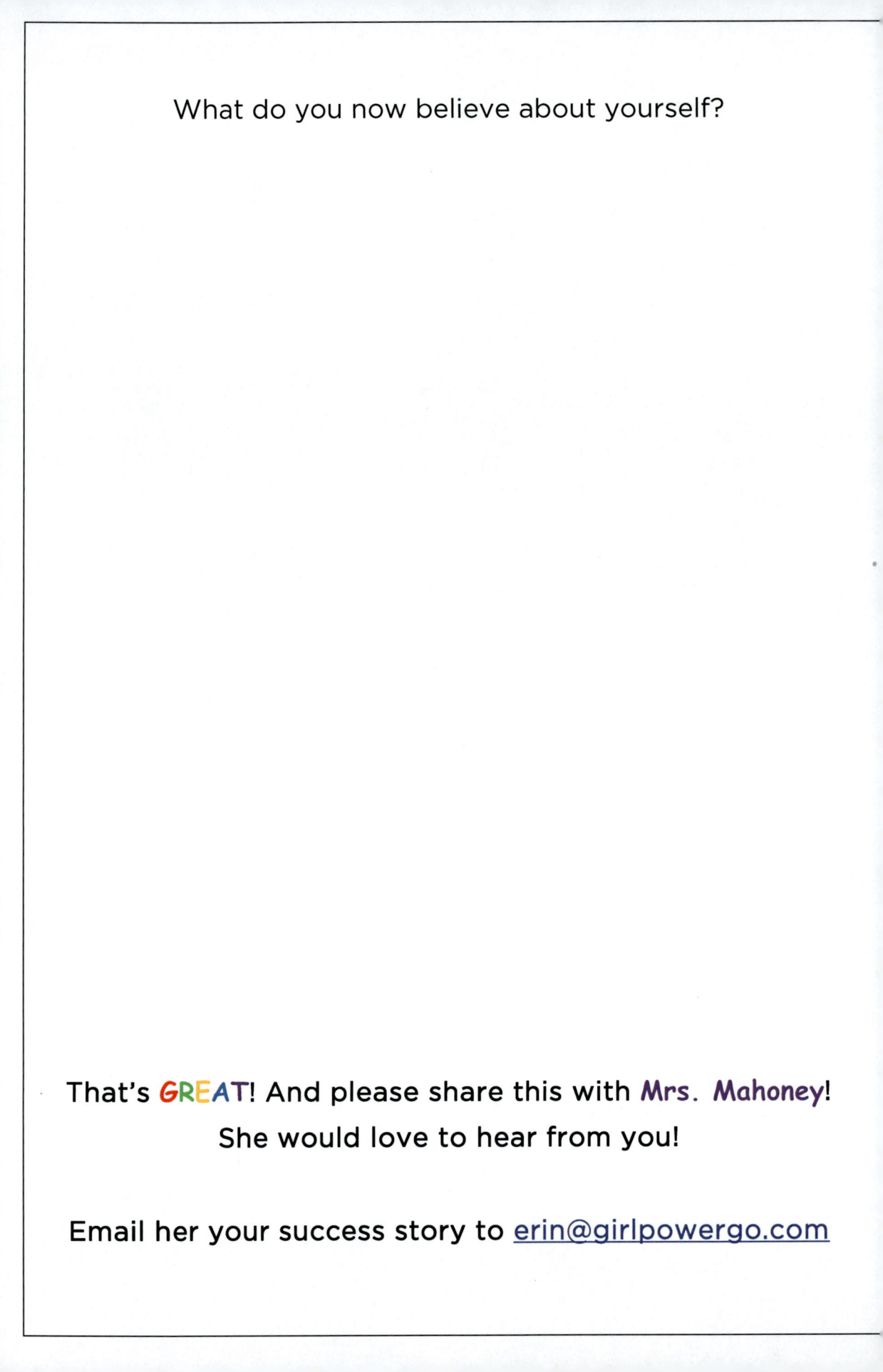

That's GREAT! And please share this with Mrs. Mahoney! She would love to hear from you!

Email her your success story to erin@girlpowergo.com

BOOKS BY ERIN C. MAHONEY

GIRL POWER GUIDEBOOK FOR PARENTS AND INSTRUCTORS: THE PROGRAM, STRATEGIES AND INSIGHTS THAT TRANSFORM AND EMPOWER GIRLS

GIRL POWER JOURNAL: BE STRONG. BE SMART. BE AMAZING!

GET MORE GIRL POWER!

Bring Girl Power programs to your community or area!

Get cool Girl Power gear!

See ongoing live and online Girl Power programs

for young girls and women!

Become a Girl Power Go Certified Instructor!

Attend a Girl Power Conference or Retreat,

Meet Erin, and learn empowerment strategies

directly from her and her team!

Go to www.GirlPowerGo.com/Extras and get updated information and news, see videos of actual Girl Power classes, and get even more positive Girl Power vibes!

IMPORTANT

The information in this book is meant to supplement, not replace, proper training. As with any sport involving speed, equipment, balance and environmental factors, there may be some inherent risk. The authors and publisher advise readers to take full responsibility for their safety and that of the girls instructed, and to also know their limits. Before practicing the skills described in this book, be sure that your equipment is well maintained, and do not take risks beyond your girls' level of experience, aptitude, training, and comfort level.

Manufactured by Amazon.com
Columbia, SC
07 April 2017